Tales of a Sea Gypsy

Ray Jason

Paradise Cay Publications

Paradise Cay Publications
P.O. Box 29
Arcata, CA 95518-0029
(800) 736-4509
(707) 822-9063 int. voice
(707) 822-9163 fax
paracay@humboldt1.com
www.paracay.com

Library of Congress Cataloguing
In Publication Data
Jason, Ray, 1946-
 Tales of a Sea Gypsy
 1. Sailing Stories
        I. Titles

ISBN 0939837471
LC Number 2001 132682
Manufactured in the United States of America

The author wishes to thank *Latitude 38* and *Cruising World* for previously publishing some of these stories in slightly different form.

Cover photo: Ray Jason and *Aventura* near Fort Jefferson at the Dry Tortugas National Park in the Florida Keys. *Photo by* Clyde Sanda

Author's photo by Hillary Adams

FOR MY MOM

She abandoned her own wanderlust
in order to dedicate her life to her five children.
That nurturing sacrifice allowed
my gypsy spirit to soar.
In hundreds of ports and half a hundred
countries, her quiet lessons
of compassion, humor and courage
have smoothed this vagabond's Path.

Contents

Introduction

How lucky could a sailor get? For the third night in a row I was being torpedoed! But these underwater missiles were not dangerous. They were just harmless, playful dolphins that were speeding over for a full-moon visit. The trails that they carved through the phosphorescent sea created the illusion that I was being torpedoed from six directions at once.

But tonight there was something unusual about their luminescent paths. Instead of playing in the bow wave like they normally do, they were tracing circles around my boat. And as they passed by only a few feet away, they would pivot their bodies and look up at me with one eye. It seemed like they were trying to communicate something.

Yet even though I hail from that wackiest of homeports, San Francisco, I had still not mastered inter-species telepathy. So their message kept eluding me until finally I looked astern and saw it emblazoned across the midnight sky. They were introducing me to my very first moonbow! Its pale silver and purple arch shimmered across the horizon and etched itself onto my sea-gypsy soul. And after I had shouted my thanks to the dolphins, I quietly said to myself, "This is why I go to sea."

But it's not the *main* reason. Mostly I go for the yarns. Landsmen hardly ever tell stories any more. They seem to limit their conversations to regurgitation of what they saw on television or read in the newspaper. But every day in the cruising world there are sailors beginning a tale with that tantalizing phrase, "Hey, have I got a good one!" And, hopefully, as you voyage through the stories in this book you will repeatedly find yourself saying, "Hey, that was a good one!"

Admittedly, none of the sailors who wander these pages was ever forced to walk the plank. And nobody prowls the decks on a pegleg. But even though they might differ from the pirates and misfits who enliven the classic sea stories of Conrad, Stevenson, and Melville, their tales are still packed with excitement, adventure, and humor.

So hoist the jib on your armchair, and come sail away with us. You'll explore a seaside ghost town, learn the correlation between pancakes and the Truth, search the night-black sea for an overboard cat, discover that all loaves of bread are not created equal, play bumper boats in the Panama Canal, uncover the secret of sailing serenity from a High Seas Master, experience the terror of a sudden sinking, and savor many other amazing escapades.

As for my own Path to the Sea, it has been marked by some eccentric but pleasant course changes. In college, I was one of those 'most likely to succeed' types. I was president of the student body, editor of the newspaper, and captain of the debate team. My college honored me by choosing me to compete for a Rhodes Scholarship.

But instead of succeeding, I ended up seceding - at least from the Real World. Vietnam had something to do with that. I was headed for law school after college, but got drafted. My tour of duty on an ammunition ship in Vietnam helped foster my love of the immense majesty and malice of the sea. But that wartime experience also affected me in another way. It profoundly undermined my capacity to trust the rhetoric of political, religious, and economic leaders.

So when I returned from Vietnam, I left the mainstream and opted for the contrary-to-ordinary tributary. People were just starting to perform on the streets in San Francisco. There were magicians, mimes, musicians, and a whole cornucopia of amazing and wondrous entertainers. But there were no jugglers. I had learned basic juggling as a teenager, so my plan was to put together a little act and give it a try for a while. That was in 1971. And I'm still at it - tossing around torches, machetes, and bowling balls.

Along the way, there have been many wonderful milestones. In the early days, the San Francisco police would run me off and even arrest me. But eventually the pioneer street performers were no longer viewed as nuisances; they became minor folk heroes. In fact, in July 1981, the mayor actually proclaimed a day in my honor. Since I love San Francisco so much, with its beauty, diversity, artistic energy, and tolerance, this civic award meant a great deal to me.

One of my other performing highlights was my Around the World journey, on which I traveled with just a backpack and a bag of tricks. I juggled on the Trans-Siberian Railway, the Great Wall of China, and the exotic Weekend Market, in Bangkok. Having left the United States with $4,000, I returned about a year later with $4,400, having passed my hat in dozens of countries.

Then, in the mid-1980s, my life's course changed again. It dawned on me that I could fulfill my long-dormant dream of wandering the world in my own small sailboat, and finance my voyaging by performing my show and selling occasional magazine stories. After all, my entire act fits into a couple of duffel bags and juggling is a universal language. So I diligently learned to sail and also mastered the old-fashioned skills of coastal piloting and celestial navigation. Then I spent a year searching for the ideal boat, which turned out to be a Farallon 29. I named her *Aventura*, the Spanish word for adventure.

And now, 20,000 miles later - most of them single-handed - I still love the cruising life. So many facets of it resonate with my truest self: its slow pace, its unpredictability, its simplicity, its wonderful fraternity of cruisers, and its intimate connection to unbridled nature. All of these elements combine into a rhapsody that soothes and pleases me. And perhaps, most importantly, on an almost daily basis the sea-gypsy life is *great fun!*

Midnight Manna

Finally I was about to meet the Mellow Mariner. In port after port along Central America's sunset shore, fellow sailors had spoken almost reverently about him. Nobody knew his real name, but when another cruiser had dubbed him Maximum Mellow, the name Max had stuck. As a seagoing yarn wrangler, I just had to learn the story of how he had achieved his legendary calm.

Our rendezvous could not have occurred at a more exotic and appropriate spot than Isla Gitana (Gypsy Island) in Costa Rica's Gulf of Nicoya. As I sailed up the channel I was treated to a schoolboy's dream of how a jungle island should look. It was as if Robert Louis Stevenson had risen from the dead to hire on as design consultant.

The level terrain on the mostly hilly island was aflutter with rustling coconut palms. Projecting through this swaying canopy was an enormous, cone-shaped palapa bar. Its height was much greater than its diameter and the spoke-like supporting branches that radiated out from the centerpost were a marvel of 'hope for the best' engineering. Upon seeing it, any first-world building inspector would probably change his cocktail order to a double and then move out from underneath the structure to drink it.

Adjacent to the palapa was the pool, and adjacent to the pool was the lifeguard, Minky the monkey. He was one of those smart, playful, white-faced monkeys that organ grinders favor. And speaking of organ grinding, some of the best entertainment on the island was provided by Minky when he would occasionally try to mount Gorda the coatimundi. This exotic animal is already a cross between a raccoon and an anteater, so it didn't need to also be crossed with a monkey. But don't try to convince Minky of that.

There was also an odd and ugly chicken named Barfly that had apparently found a testosterone bush somewhere on the island. This would explain her aggressive behavior. Unlike all of the other chickens, which were confined to egg-laying duties in the hen house, Barfly's turf was the circular bar beneath the palapa. And if Rocky, the baby raccoon, wandered in, this Rambo hen would chase it until the poor, frightened creature ran up the nearest human body and perched on its shoulder like a parrot. Upon seeing this, Rico the real parrot, would get jealous and start repeating, "Rocky bad, Rocky bad, Rocky bad!" With free entertainment like this, provided by this motley menagerie, happy hours were never dull, and nobody complained that there was no satellite dish with 50 channels.

The island is owned and operated by a 79-year-old American named Carl, who apparently had also found the local testosterone bush. That would explain his recent marriage to Loida, his 32-year-old Philippine bride. This fun-loving, female firecracker could speak three languages and cook in five. Rounding out Isla Gitana's hale and hospitable crew were Shawna, Carl T, and Finn.

Shawna is the owner's granddaughter and even though she was only sweet sixteen, she could bartend with the best of them. It was tough to name a drink that she couldn't mix, either in English or Spanish. Carl T is the proprietor's nephew. What the T stood for I never learned, but it might have been for Tough. He had to be Tough with a capital T in order to go for his frequent swims in the bay. That's because each month during the highest tides the anchorage would look like driftwood stew, and yet Carl T would plow through it like some sort of tropical, human icebreaker.

Finn had jumped ship at the island. His former skipper had the endearing habit of kicking him to wake him up for watch. Finn, who is a large, healthy specimen, could have easily booted the brute a boat length. But being a gentle person, he chose discretion over kickback and cast his lot with Isla Gitana's exotic fauna. Of course, I didn't learn all of this about the isla's inhabitants until later. However, since everyone there is so relaxed and friendly, in no time at all you feel like you've known them for years.

As I rowed past the Mellow Mariner's 32-footer, I chuckled at her name, *Maybe Thursday*. That's because I had already learned through the sailor's grapevine, also known as the coconut telegraph, that his dinghy is named *Maybe Not* and his kayak is dubbed *Maybe Never*. Ashore, I was pleasantly greeted by a few cruisers who had already crossed tacks with *Aventura* in some port or some storm. A cold beer was handed to me and we all lifted our drinks in the Costa Rican toast of "pura vida!" This literally means "pure life," but it also means "to the good life," And that certainly makes sense; for many wayfaring sailors believe that the good life has to include a certain amount of impurity, perhaps even a goodly amount of impurity.

Finally, I was introduced to Max. His first words to me may not have been mellow, but they were definitely memorable: "I see you don't have any inflatable pajamas."

As a 20-year veteran street performer, where ad-libs and comeback lines go with the territory, I responded, "No, I don't. But there have been times when some inflatable pajama bottoms would have come in handy."

We all laughed and somebody explained to me that the cloth covers that many cruisers attach to their dinghies in order to lessen sun damage, are what Max meant by "inflatable pajamas." Since I own an ancient Avon Redcrest that has escaped tubular meltdown for 15 years and 20,000 miles, I shared Max's disparaging opinion of this item. They strike me as a classic example of a 'foolish luxury becoming a bogus necessity.' Max continued the conversation by asking me if I always rowed my dinghy.

"Yep, *Ling* has never been defiled with an outboard. I'm in no hurry. I may be money poor, but I'm time-rich."

"Did I hear you say that your dinghy is named *Ling*? That's a rather odd choice."

"Oh, not really," I replied. "Don't you remember that old bawdy song with the chorus that went, oh my dinghy Ling, my dinghy Ling, my dinghy Ling is the cutest thing?"

This cracked up sailor and sailorette alike. When we all stopped laughing, I asked Max if he had ever used an outboard.

"Yes I have, but not any more. That was in the old days, before my epiphany at the Panama Canal. However, that's part of a long story, a long sea story."

"Don't forget, Max, I'm time-rich and I'd love to hear it."

"Yes, but when I say sea story I also mean a tale best told at sea. However, if you would like to sail me to Tamarindo, I would gladly regale you with the entire saga."

"But Max, I've just come from there. Why this great craving to go to Tamarindo, and why don't you take *Maybe Thursday*?"

"The saltwater pump on my engine is blown, so I can't motor, and the headboard on my main ripped out, so I can't sail. In the meantime I've got a buyer in Tamarindo that I don't want to lose."

A certain euphoric agricultural product sprang to mind as his possible merchandise. I had my suspicions, but wanting to give him the benefit of the doubt I replied, "And what kind of exotic goods might you be wishing to share with the good citizens of Tamarindo, Maxo Polo?"

"I have a mint condition long board that a rich, Swiss surfer wants to buy. I'll give you a hundred bucks from the profits for helping me."

This was starting to get tempting. I could earn some cruising money, hear Max's life change saga, and meet what certainly must be an endangered species, a Swiss surfer. "Okay, Max, it's a deal - if you can wait a couple of days to leave. I'd like to hang here and relax a bit. I've got a hunch that this might be a very magical little island."

Several tides later we were riding a strong ebb out of the Gulf of Nicoya. We skirted the unmarked rock that had taken a *Jaws*-sized bite out of a Fisher 37 named *Ida Z*. A suitcase-sized chunk of her hull now adorns the Isla Gitana palapa bar. At Bahia Ballena we passed the unfortunate CSY 44 that has been abandoned, and now serves as a pelican sanctuary and guano plantation. Rounding Cabo Blanco, we searched the shoreline for the remains of a Japanese car carrier that had met her end nearby. Because it was dusk, we were unable to spot her. So I'll never know whether the wreck of the *Screwuppo Maru* is just another sailor's myth. The beautiful sunset and our passage from gulf to ocean were the catalyst that Max needed to tell me the yarn that I had yearned for, the tale of his transformation.

It began at the Balboa Yacht Club on the Pacific side of the Panama Canal. For many years it had been his dream to transit the canal and idle away in the western Caribbean. The San Blas Islands, Roatan, Belize, and the Rio Dulce - their names alone quickened his pulse and pulled at his anchor. But just when he was on the threshold of realizing his dream, the Sky Bosun intervened.

Since Max would need to motor his boat through long stretches of the canal, he undertook a preventive maintenance program on his aging diesel. He installed a new impeller, changed the oil and filter, replaced the thermostat, and decided to inspect the fuel injectors. He did not decide to drop one of them, but that is what happened. And it landed directly on its tip, thus destroying it from now to eternity.

So he had to order a new one from California. It was supposed to take one or two weeks but ended up being nearly a month. He tried to lessen the frustration of this delay by ordering some other items from the States that he couldn't buy locally. Finally, everything cleared Customs and he was happily rolling his stack of boxes toward the Balboa Yacht Club dock in one of the carts that they provide. These are basically wooden boxes on wheels with a long, U-shaped handle made out of aluminum tubing.

The tidal range there is extreme, so the ramp to the dock is a long one. When the tide is low, this ramp is also steep. Very steep. Steeper than credit card interest rates. Midway down the ramp, the handle suddenly broke off from the cart and Max watched his precious cargo roll down the incline, across the dock and into the muddy, swift-flowing water.

At this point one might expect cries of anguish or rage. Instead,

Max walked quietly to the edge of the dock and pointed the rotten aluminum handle at the spot where everything had sunk. He stood frozen in this position for minutes. To someone passing by, he must have looked like a demented medicine man with an oddly shaped dowsing stick, trying to find dry where there is only wet.

Music brought him out of his trance. A small workboat passing nearby was playing the song *Cast Your Fate to the Wind*. To Max it seemed like the lyrics to the song were a special delivery message intended just for his ears, telling him that it was not yet his time to cross over to the islands of his desires.

So he went back. He changed his exit zarpe from Roatan to Costa Rica, arranged for another injector to be shipped to Puntarenas, and waited for a favorable breeze. This was the first time he had ever attempted a lengthy passage without his engine as backup, but since he was casting his fate to the wind, it didn't matter anyway.

He also realized that if he could change his destination so dramatically, he could also change his attitude. His personal quest would be to no longer sweat the small stuff. He renamed his boat *Maybe Thursday*, which summed up his new, carefree attitude towards departures and arrivals. His motto became 'Why worry at a banquet?' Because he realized that even when totally becalmed, if one remains alert and observant there is still a whole lot going on in the sea, in the sky, in the library.

Amazingly enough, he was not becalmed, except philosophically. In fact, it seemed like the forces of nature were rewarding him for this new tack in his life's course. A favorable current nudged him northward; a warm, manageable wind caressed his sails, and a celestial circus entertained him. He saw double rainbows, meteor showers, and even a rare, pale lavender moonbow.

In the water there were booby birds convening on the backs of gigantic sea turtles. During the nights, dolphins sped towards his hull like torpedoes of phosphorescent, squeaking joy. And his favorite visitation came from a mother manta ray and her newborn. The majestic, eight-foot wide mom was teaching the youngster the pleasure of swimming in the border of light and shadow that a sailboat casts. Each new treasure reinforced his determination to retool his life so that he would worry less and enjoy more.

"Has it been difficult to sustain that maximum mellow attitude?" I asked him, when it was clear that his story was beginning to wind down.

"Of course it is sometimes, but cruising is certainly one of the most ideal lifestyles for fostering tranquility. And every time that I am tempted to lose my composure, I remember how transient my problems are and how everlasting are my memories of that moonbow and those mantas. I also keep myself in line by regular use of the *purgatorio.*"

"The what?" I said.

"The oven on a small sailboat. Also known as the *saunacator* because of the way it heats up the cabin. And by the way, can I use yours now? On the first night at sea it's a nice ritual, plus it means delicious bread on the night watches."

"Sounds great. But let me show you how to ignite the pilot light. It's a bit quirky."

By 2300 we were enjoying the carbos of his labor. Since the breeze had died down we were sitting on *Aventura's* foredeck to lessen the diesel noise while we savored the warm, delicious bread.

We both spotted the lights at the same time. Green and red with no separation between them.

"Must be a masthead tricolor light," said Max.

"Yep, looks like we've got another sailboat in the neighborhood," I added. "Shall we chat 'em up on the radio?"

"Absolutely. I'm sure they wouldn't mind a little conversation to speed along a night watch."

But no one responded.

"They're getting pretty close now," said Max, who had moved astern to the cockpit. "We'd better alter course."

Which we did. We also gave them some very loud blasts with the air horn. Still there was no response from the oncoming sloop.

"This is beginning to piss me off, Max."

"Relax," he responded. "Have you got a spotlight?"

"You bet, and it's a strong one. It could melt the chrome off a winch handle."

So we ground zeroed them. But, amazingly, no head popped out of the cabin.

"Max, how can any self-respecting ocean sailor keep such a shabby watch? I feel like motoring right up beside them and blasting them with the light and the horn at the same time."

"Go ahead and ease up beside them, but I've got a better idea than blasting them," suggested Max.

Then he went below. When he returned he was carrying the other fresh loaf of bread.

"As close as you can," whispered Max. "But do it quietly."

When we were only a few feet away, he gently tossed the loaf of bread into the offending sailboat's cockpit. I eased the helm down and we returned to our original course. Max's smile was both mischievous and beatific.

"You are mellow indeed," I said to him. "I would have never thought of that."

"Well, sometimes it's better to spook a sailor into watchfulness than blast him."

"Sounds like a good theory to me." I answered.

"It's more than just theory," said Max. "I once found a loaf of midnight manna in my cockpit!"

Dance Therapy

When their house got eaten, they knew it was time to go to sea. Anne and Bill were well aware of the diabolical reputation of the Texas termite; so before they bought their split-level ranch home, they had it carefully inspected. But apparently an army of wood locusts had been hibernating so deeply in the ground beneath the house that the inspector failed to notice them. Either that, or he had an uncle in the sawdust business.

The exterminators labored valiantly, but the infestation was just too immense. The macabre scene transfixed their horrified neighbors, as huge, bloated garbage bags full of dead termites were carried to the backyard and burned. The surrealism of the picture was surpassed only by the stench of the pyre. But it was a lost cause and a lost casa. Within a week, the 2 x 4 framing had been reduced to the thickness of a pencil. And then it just collapsed in on itself like a paper house made out of S & L shares.

Weary of their land luck, Anne and Bill took the insurance money and went looking for a sailboat. Their requirements were simple - any seaworthy vessel would do as long as it wasn't made out of *wood*. In San Diego they found a fine 40-footer and moved aboard. They spent the spring and summer in the light, forgiving breezes off Point Loma learning how to sail. In the fall, they attended the big beach party that the Downwind Marine yacht chandlery puts on for each year's southbound sailors.

They went to this gathering of the cruising clan because the following year they hoped to sail to *mañanaland* themselves. They figured that it would take about 12 more months until their skills were solid enough to make the big jump. But fate figured otherwise. For at the cruiser's party they met at least four couples who seemed to have even less knowledge about voyaging than they did. And so the euphoria of the day, combined with their inflated assessment of their skill level, convinced Anne and Bill that they needn't wait another year. Possibly the unholy marriage of Margarita and Captain Morgan also factored into this bold but foolish decision.

A month later they cast off the docklines. A month and two days later, they're already in trouble. Big trouble. The kind where Bill is writhing around on the cabin sole in extreme pain. On land, Anne had never been a great cook, but certainly her first few meals at sea weren't bad enough to merit this sort of reaction. She repeatedly asked him what was wrong, but he could only cradle his stomach and mutter, "I known't dough." Since Bill had never been dyslexic before, except when he won at bingo, she knew that this was very serious.

They had planned to discuss various emergency tactics as soon as they crossed into Mexican waters on their first day at sea, but the dockside farewell party had worn them out. On the second day, the wind and wave conditions were rougher than expected so this vital conversation got postponed again. But now a dialogue was impossible and Anne had to think for herself and fend for both of them.

She knew that they were in foreign waters. And she knew that they were having an emergency. So she did the natural thing - she called American Express. Their platinum card included air medical evacuation amongst its various services. This was not a free perk; in fact, it was enormously expensive. But dollars were dimes at a time like this.

Reaching American Express is no simple matter when one is 25 miles off the Mexican coast. It's not like she could just call down to the concierge and ask her to ring up the office. But she had started studying for her ham radio license a few weeks earlier. And even though Morse code still made about as much sense to her as Bosnian Karaoke, she at least knew how to turn on the receiver and use the microphone.

Meanwhile, near Waycross, Georgia, a black subsistence farmer was just turning on his ham radio set. It was the one re-maining joy in his 'tired of livin' but scared of dyin' existence. He had been a radio operator during his Air Force tour of duty in Vietnam. Since that had been the only time in his life that he had ever left the country, it had soured him on foreign travel. But he loved to wander the world via the airwaves.

The first thing he heard that rainy night in Waycross, was a panicked woman repeating, "Mae West, Mae West, Mae West." He keyed his transmitter, gave his call sign, and then asked calmly, "Ma'am, are you meanin' to say Mayday?"

"Why yes. Oh, how ditsy of me. Who am I talking to?"

"This is James George Jackson in Waycross, Georgia, but my radio name is Farmer Jim. Are you in trouble, ma'am?"

"Yes I am, Farmer John."

"That's Farmer Jim, ma'am."

"Sorry, I'm a little panicked. You see my husband and I are in our yacht off the coast of Mexico and we desperately need your help. Would you please call American Express and ask them to send us a helicopter?"

"Why the hurry, ma'am? Can't you wait until you get back to land to buy yourselves a helicopter?"

"No, no, I don't want to buy one. My husband is terribly sick and needs to be rescued."

"Oh, air medevac," said the Vietnam vet.

"Yes, Farmer Jim. I need a helicopter to pick him up and take him to the hospital in Ensenada."

"Give me the number and I'll call the credit card folks for you. But you best tell me what's wrong with him. They're sure gonna wanna know."

"He had extreme abdominal pain and then he passed out."

"Uh oh. That could be a mess a things - 'pendicitis, bleedin' ulcer, kidney stones. I'll get right on it. Now you stay there while I make a phone call or two."

It actually took four before he reached the person who handled overseas medical emergencies. And it took that agent another three calls until he had an air medevac outfit in San Diego ready to launch. They just needed one more thing and then the rescue could begin.

"Yacht ma'am, yacht ma'am, yacht ma'am, this is Farmer Jim. Do you read me."

"Yes, Farmer Jim, loud and clear. Did you have any luck?"

"Some luck, some skill. We got a whirly ready to scramble in San Diego. The American Express fella just needs your credit card number."

At this point, some deeply entrenched upper-class female-shopper switch clicked on and shorted out all of Anne's normal reasoning faculties. Call it the Neiman-Marcus solenoid if you will. Anyway, she sputtered into the microphone, "But I can't give out my number over the air. It's a platinum card. You never know who might be listening. I'll give them my name and address and they can look up my number in their computer."

"Ma'am, this fella has been plenty helpful so far, but I don't think he's gonna like this. Stand by and I'll check."

While Farmer Jim talked with the American Express agent, Anne knelt down to see if she could rouse Bill back to consciousness. Not only was she unable to do that, but she also discovered that he seemed to have stopped breathing. Immediately, another subconscious solenoid kicked in, this one far more rational and helpful. She was instantly able to recall her CPR training from that 'first-aid-for-tornado-victims class' she had taken back in Texas.

Well, not only did it work; it produced spectacular results. Although she was not aware of it, Bill had just passed a kidney stone, which transports the victim from the land of death-wish agony to glades of heaven-on-earth bliss. So not only was he awakening free of pain, but his wife was kissing him and pressing his chest with a fervor that he hadn't experienced in years. "Ain't cruisin' grand?" he thought to himself.

Meanwhile, Anne realized that Bill's mouth had gone from lifeless to hot, devouring, and passionate. And then his arms embraced her and they rolled around on the cabin floor like two teenagers in a pickup truck with a shell top. As they were carnally cavorting, the ham radio began to crackle with the voice of Farmer

Jim trying to contact her. Finally she heard his repeated calls, peeled herself off her husband and said, "Hello, Farmer Tim."

"That's Farmer Jim, ma'am. Is everything okay? Your voice sounds different."

"Oh yes, everything's fine," she said, trying to catch her breath. "Everything's glorious!"

"So you mean you won't be needin' the helicopter, ma'am?"

"Of course not. Who needs a helicopter on a honeymoon?"

While the kind-hearted farmer sat there trying to solve the riddle of her last statement, she suddenly realized how absurd it must have sounded and said, "Farmer Jim, whatever was wrong with my husband suddenly went away. He's fine now. But I want to thank you for your help. Please give me your address and I'll send you a little present when we get to port."

"Oh, you needn't do that, yacht ma'am."

"Well, maybe I don't need to, but I want to, and I will."

So he gave her his information and they ended their conversation. Then Farmer Jim walked out to the little front porch of his Georgia farmhouse and looked up at the stars and quietly pondered the magic that is shortwave radio, and the mystery that is Life.

The next few days were sailing at its best. A mild northwesterly breeze of about 12 knots gently eased them down the Baja coast while the stark desert scenery dazzled them. Conditions were mild enough that they felt comfortable staying only a couple of miles offshore. After their near catastrophe, they decided that they would find a qualified doctor amongst the large American community in Cabo San Lucas. Since Bill had no prior history of kidney stones, they didn't know much about them.

Unfortunately, before they made it to Cabo they would learn more. The pains started shortly after dawn. Initially, they weren't as severe as the first attack, so Bill searched the charts for a nearby anchorage with a town that might have a doctor. About six miles down the coast was the sizable village of Abreojos. They were encouraged by the fact that it had an airstrip, and discouraged by the size of the waves breaking on the beach. Their cruising guide added to their concern with its admonishment to 'practice your initial surf landing elsewhere.'

But the pain was starting to build so fiercely that drowning in a pounding shorebreak sounded like an appealing option. Getting the boat anchored was the last task that Bill could assist with. He could only mumble instructions to Anne as she pumped up and launched the dinghy. Attaching the heavy outboard motor without his help was out of the question, so she would have to row them both ashore.

Putting a hot dog in a parking meter would have been easier than dumping her limp, contorted husband into the inflatable, but amazingly she managed it. However, her attempt to row them through the surf line was gallant but doomed. First they sloshed, then they submarined, and finally they somersaulted. But by the time they were ejected from the dinghy, they were only in knee-deep water, and Bill was able to crawl up the beach toward the most substantial building that he saw. He made it to the doorway where he blabbered something that sounded like "Hease plelp me." And then he passed out.

But again they had caught a lucky break. The very building that delirium had guided him to was a modest but clean medical clinic. Furthermore, it was run by a young woman doctor from Mexico City. She was required to work in a rural facility for a couple of years as a way of paying the government back for helping to send her to medical school. Anne learned all of this shortly after she managed to collect the dinghy and oars, which had gone in separate directions when they cartwheeled ashore. By the time she reached the tiny infirmary, Bill's wet clothes had been removed and he had been injected with painkiller and a sedative. He was sleeping peacefully beneath a clean, lightweight blanket.

After the doctor questioned Anne about her husband's symptoms and medical history, they settled in and got better acquainted. Carmina particularly enjoyed the opportunity to speak English, which she had rarely done since leaving medical school. After a few hours, Bill started to wake up. When he began to move, the doctor lifted him into the seated position and started punching him in the lower back. This helps a kidney stone clear the system.

In his dazed and drugged condition, he awoke to this assault thinking, 'Where am I? Who is this sadistic woman? And why does she hate me?' Then he noticed his wife beside him. And rather than protecting him from this señorita de Sade, she seemed to be whispering, "It's OK, it's OK." Well, it might be OK in some parallel universe, but it was the pits in this present one. And speaking of pits, a few minutes later he passed another kidney stone. Again his relief was instantaneous and euphoric, perhaps even more so this time because of the Demerol coursing through his bloodstream.

Anne now introduced the doctor, and explained the situation to Bill. He thanked Carmina profusely and said that if there was anything he could do for her, to just ask. Hearing this, Anne said, "There is something, dear. Carmina and I were talking while you were resting and she told me that the thing she misses most about being stationed in a tiny, isolated village like this is *dancing*. Back in Mexico City that was one of her great joys in life. Honey, perhaps you could dance with her."

And then the doctor gazed at him with her beautiful, brown eyes and made him an offer that not many mortals could refuse: "If I give you another shot of Demerol, will you dance with me?"

The Secret Ingredient

Of course I was frightened. After all, the man who had attempted this before me did not come back alive. And even though I tried to submerge the memory of his tragedy, it eerily floated to the surface only a few hours after my voyage began.

The challenge facing me was my qualifying sail for the 1990 Singlehanded TransPac race from San Francisco to the Hawaiian island of Kauai. I had to complete a 400-mile course that took me at least 100 miles offshore. Additionally, I was required to use only celestial navigation. Afterward, the race committee would examine sextant readings, worksheets, and calculations. Naturally, I was not allowed to use my engine.

During all of the previous Singlehanded TransPacs no sailor had ever been killed or even seriously injured. But two racers had died during their qualifying sails. The first one had occurred several years before, but the second had happened only a few weeks earlier. His boat was found drifting, and there was no sign of the skipper. The mainsail was partially raised, and it appeared that he had fallen overboard while attempting to reduce the size of his sails during some rough weather.

Although I didn't know the man, I felt the bond that all solo ocean sailors share, and so I was deeply saddened by his loss. I was also profoundly sobered by the chilling vision of him being suddenly overboard, watching his boat sail away while his autopilot steered. But I couldn't let his misfortune undermine my determination. However, before leaving, I posted Three Golden Rules by my chart table:

1. Stay on the boat.
2. Leave the water on the outside.
3. Keep the heavy side down.

I chose San Francisco's Indian summer for my attempt. My hope was to slip between the strong northwesterly winds of the summer and the stormy southwesterlies of winter. If I got lucky, I might also miss the last of the summer fog. But in this respect, I didn't get lucky. In fact, in every respect I didn't get lucky. That day I seemed destined to be about as unlucky as Quasimodo at a singles bar.

My first nemesis was a Navy helicopter carrier. As I was leaving Pier 39, where my lovely sloop *Aventura* was berthed, I noticed this ship preparing to depart her dock adjacent to Fisherman's Wharf.

Since there was a strong flood tide flowing in through the Golden Gate, my plan was to short-tack in a zig-zag pattern up the cityfront to lessen the effect of the unfavorable current. But the tugboats were starting to pull the carrier away from the wharf. To avoid collision on the starboard tack, I would have to pile *Aventura* up onto Jefferson Street, where she could be the day's featured attraction at Ripley's Believe It or Not Museum. Port tack would send me out toward Alcatraz and the Current Without Pity.

It took hours for me to finally work my way back to the city side of the bay. As I now sailed toward the Golden Gate Bridge, I noticed my second adversary. The fog was beginning to peek over the hills of Marin County. And it wasn't just peeking; it was smirking. This made the south side of the entrance even more desirable. If I could just get out to the Mile Rock tower before the fog obscured the main ship channel, I would feel a lot more comfortable.

But at this point my years of living dangerously finally caught up to me. A third foe was gaining on me from astern - the Coast Guard. Apparently, they were able to sense telepathically that I had been living the life of a heinous criminal. They somehow knew that my 'Discharge of Oil Overboard is Prohibited' placard was not prominently displayed near my engine room. If I was capable of such a vile offense, there was no telling what other deeds I might perpetrate against an unwary citizenry. This called for a 'safety inspection.'

They approached me in a large, fast inflatable boat and instructed me to drop my sails and motor back toward the city. I explained that I was trying to qualify for an important, well-respected race to Hawaii, and that it was against the rules for me to engage my engine. Their next suggestion was for me to heave to, or essentially stall the boat out. But this would sweep me back toward Alcatraz. So I selected the third option which was to hold my course while they came aboard and conducted their inspection. The problem with this last choice was that it was sailing me into both the fog and the nasty section of the main shipping channel just beneath the Golden Gate Bridge.

Ironically, in my 15 years of sailing San Francisco Bay, the

Coast Guard had never boarded me. At this point a little voice, a sort of Jiminy Crustacean, whispered to me that the bad omens were starting to pile up. Perhaps tomorrow would be a better day to begin this undertaking. But after the USCG determined that my only offense was the missing oil-discharge placard, I continued on my way. I tacked *Aventura* onto starboard in hopes of outrunning the fog that had now nearly overtaken me. But my bad luck continued, and instead I just escorted the White Peril over to the south side of the channel.

However, my luck was about to change. But not from bad to good. It went instead from grim to gruesome. I nearly ran over a 'floater' - a dead body in the water. An inbound Navy tugboat passed very close to me. Seconds later I heard them radio the Coast Guard that they had found a dead person in the water. I must have practically sailed right over the drifting corpse.

In the fog I never saw it. But in my mind's eye, I watched the fallen singlehander float by me and warn me to turn back and abandon this foolish and deadly quest. I was shaken and staggered by this confrontation. My confidence sank as low as the keel on the *Titanic*. The next few miles were sailed on emotional autopilot. I was struggling hard to maintain the courage to continue.

Fortunately, my morale got a boost from the radio a little while later. The crew from the Navy tug found some identification and a suicide note on the body. It was not the missing solo sailor. It was someone who had jumped from the Golden Gate Bridge. My concentration could now return to the matter at hand. This was an excellent time to regain such focus because I couldn't see a damned thing. The fog was now as thick as a Rush Limbaugh baloney sandwich. And not only was it thick, it was also jam-packed full of ships.

Since I couldn't afford radar, I was monitoring the Vessel

Traffic Control channel to find out who was in the neighborhood. Fleet Week had just ended in San Francisco, so there was an entire Navy convoy headed out. Inbound were a tanker, a cruise ship, and a pilot boat. Plus there was a Coast Guard buoy tender meandering around doing maintenance work. Who wasn't in the neighborhood? I was half expecting Mr. Rogers to come paddling by in a kayak.

The buoy tender soon became my next crisis. I was short-tacking just south of the narrow channel that cuts through the dangerous shallow waters known as the Potato Patch. Since electronic navigation was not permitted during this qualifying sail, and since I didn't own such equipment anyway, my strategy was to stay close to the eight buoys that mark this channel and then head to Southeast Farallon Island. Once I was west of that I would be into open ocean and things would be a lot less stressful.

Trying to keep those buoys in sight through the fog was forcing me to stay much closer to the ships than I preferred. During one of my tacks back toward them I saw the big buoy tender approach and overtake me. After it passed, I darted below to check my chart. The next thing I needed to check was my pulse because it went off the scale.

Returning to the cockpit, I was shocked to see that the repair ship had stopped directly in front of me. I snatched the tiller from the autopilot and pushed it hard over, executing a suicide tack without even releasing the jib sheet. As she came about with her jib backed, *Aventura* heeled over so radically that much of her bottom was exposed. It must have looked like we were mooning the Coast Guard ship. And I must admit that this thought did enter my mind, considering my two encounters with the Coasties that day. But this near miss was probably my fault for not realizing that the tender might work on the buoy directly in front of me.

Amazingly enough, all of this had taken place during the first six hours of my qualifier. I couldn't believe how much shinola I had already sailed through. At this rate I wouldn't have enough underwear to last through the whole voyage. Had a submarine surfaced under me and impaled me on its periscope, I would not have been surprised. Surely I was due for a break. Right? Not!

The fog did suddenly clear, but this just revealed how precarious my position was. There were five vessels in sight and it seemed like they all wanted to line dance with my lovely sloop. Besides this, there was now a completely unexpected nemesis in view. It looked like some kind of red river was flowing through the ocean. My first guess was that it was an oil spill. But why the blood-red color? To the best of my knowledge, even Communist tankers never carried red oil.

Perhaps a large whale had gotten run over by a ship. But that possibility seemed unlikely because there was just too much of the stuff. In fact, it was spread out over such a wide area that I was unable to avoid sailing through it. As I entered the scarlet stream, I looked down at the waterline to see if it was staining my beautiful white hull. And there I finally found it - something that I had long been searching for - the possible origin of the phrase 'grody to the max.' Because swimming around in the crimson goop were millions of jellyfish. And many of them were as big as basketballs. One glimpse at that vile stew and I immediately said to myself, "This stuff is grody to the max."

In fact, it was such an unsettling apparition that I radioed the scientists stationed at Southeast Farallon Island to see if they had some sort of explanation. Even they didn't know. They guessed that it was some sort of 'red tide.' Before signing off, they did ask if I had a 'history of flashbacks,' whatever that means.

Eventually, *Aventura* did get west of the Farallon Islands and into the wide Pacific. I felt much more at ease now that we were in open water and farther away from the shipping lanes. To celebrate this success, I fixed myself a sunset cocktail. Given the bizarre events of the day, it seemed like a stout one was in order, so I prepared an orange juice with a healthy dollop of dark rum. It was delicious, which is a word very similar to delirious, which was the way I felt when I spotted my next visitor.

It was a big sea gull, which doesn't sound like a big deal, except that it didn't fly over to visit me; it seemed to just... materialize. I was sitting in the cockpit facing aft when it suddenly appeared about 10 feet above me. And what made this apparition particularly disturbing was the fact that it wasn't flapping its wings at all. The only thing in motion was its head, which would gaze forward one moment, then stare down at me the next. This really spooked me. But how could it not, since my nerves were so jangled from all of the other tribulations that I had endured in the last 12 hours.

Just when I was about to go below to check the rum bottle to see if it smelled bad, I suddenly figured it out. My visitor was Jonathan Glidingston Seagull. He was hovering and gliding in the windstream that my mainsail was creating. I laughed at my mental slowness and then applauded the gull's performance. Unfortunately, the clapping scared him away.

As he flew off toward the horizon I noticed that the gull disappeared rather swiftly. Too swiftly. Which brought to mind the 'f' word again. Fog. Damn, would these ordeals never cease? Within an hour my visibility was again practically zero. At nightfall I switched on my masthead tricolor navigation light in hopes that it would alert any nearby ships. While sitting there wishing for a strobe light, with its much greater brightness, I suddenly remembered Terry's lifejacket. His personal strobe was still attached, and even though its battery would be dead, I had plenty of spares.

Within five minutes I had it operating and was hoisting it up the mast where it flashed out its warning.

As I settled back into the cockpit and stared at the blinking strobe, I was overwhelmed by emotion. Not because of the many traumas that I had weathered that day, but because of my memories of Terry. He was the best friend that I ever had, the only person that I ever asked to sail with me. But Fate took him early, and sent him up the River of the Nine Bends. And he would never return.

We had sailed together on *Aventura's* 1985 voyage to Mexico, Hawaii, and back to San Francisco. We were planning a second trip when he fell off that cliff in Yosemite. Had the Sky Bosun not called him to the Final Anchorage, I might have never begun my singlehanding. And now, here I was on the first night of my first real singlehanded passage. I was frightened in the fog and beaten down by a nerve-numbing string of events. But looking up at Terry's strobe gave me strength and solace. The blinking light was as bright as his smile and as sparkling as his humor. It reminded me of our first sea trial together.

We had been friends for 20 years, going all the way back to our college days. We had been partners on the debate team, which meant traveling together about 20 weekends each year competing in tournaments. Inter-collegiate debating is a pressure-packed environment, but Terry and I never had a harsh word between us. We were very compatible. So when I started planning my 1985 cruise I invited him to join me. Although his sailing experience was limited, that seemed far less important than our ability to get along well in stressful situations. After many practice sails in the Bay, we decided that it was time to test his sea legs on a three-day trip out beyond the Farallon Islands.

Terry loved to cook, and for his first evening meal he decided to whip up falafels. All day long he had displayed no signs of seasickness, but when I saw him stirring the falafel mix down in the galley, he looked a bit queasy. But since this was his first real passage he wanted to persevere. However, the sea is often stronger than the mind. He suddenly threw up with gusto directly into the bowl of falafel dough. After regaining his composure, he looked up at me with a beatific grin and said, "Damn, you saw the secret ingredient!"

As I tried to persevere through my maiden singlehanded voyage, I realized that Terry's real secret ingredient was laughter. And that if I could just maintain my sense of humor as he always did, then I could successfully complete this crazy qualifying sail. And four days later, I did.

Thanks, Terry.

Frozen Assets

"The Ziploc bag!" he shouted to his wife who was already in the liferaft. "I'm going back for it."

"No, don't, don't do it." she pleaded. "It's not worth dying for. The boat could sink at any moment and you'd get trapped inside."

But the $15,000 that he had stashed in a resealable plastic bag and hidden deep in the freezer seemed worth the risk to him. At least they'd have a little something to start over with. Like so many other cruisers, they had sold everything to buy their dreamboat. So when it would soon slip beneath the surface on its solitary slide to deep death, it would carry all of their possessions. He had to get to that plastic bag filled with both hundreds and hope. He had to keep the sea devil from savoring a total victory.

In the darkness he found the companionway hatch and plunged below - all too literally, for the water was above his knees. He was naked except for a bulky foul-weather jacket that he had grabbed when the impact hurled him from his bunk. In equatorial latitudes he preferred nude slumber, a penchant his wife had dubbed 'sleeping tropicale.' His bare legs made it easy for him to monitor the water's rise as he desperately flung pork chops and Popsicles out of the reefer box. He knew he was in trouble when he started to giggle. This meant that the swallowing sea was now tickling a certain sensitive sector of his anatomy.

Suddenly the boat lunged downward and to starboard. He couldn't delay any longer. He started to pull his hand out of the freezer, but the quick lurch had knocked something against his elbow. He grabbed at it. Incredible. It was a Ziploc full of green. As the deepening water ballooned out his foul-weather coat, he stuffed the bag in a big pocket and hurried up the ladder.

Once topside, his eyes quickly adjusted to the darkness. Indeed, with the faint starlight it was actually easier to see up there than it had been in the total blackness down below. His wife's terrified face stood out clearly in the doorway of the liferaft. In fact, the ghostly vividness of her features brought to mind the phrase 'white with fear.' He could plainly see that she was shouting, and as he moved down the sidedeck her words became audible: "Hurry, hurry, she's going down fast!"

And truly she was. For no sooner had he recalled the advice of an old sailing mentor only to step UP into a liferaft, than it was time to do just that. His final movement aboard their beloved sloop was more comic than heroic; more a staggering lurch than a graceful step into the flexing raft. Because of the bright yellow foul-weather jacket, his wife later described his arrival as looking like Big Bird on rollerblades.

But at the time she didn't say anything. She was too busy cutting the tether that attached them to the sailboat. Otherwise, they could be pulled beneath the waves as unwilling riders in the caboose of a deep-sea death train. Now the raft was drifting away from the mortally wounded sloop. Like a sounding whale, the stern lifted slightly as she made her final plunge.

And then she was gone - their magnificent swan of fiberglass and canvas, that had so often swelled their hearts with pride. Now there was just a profound emptiness on the vast, black ocean. Her demise had been so swift and surreal that it was as if she had never existed, as if she had been merely a shadow of an illusion of a mirage.

At this point, the overwhelming despair that they felt nearly paralyzed them. They could not move or speak or think. They could only stare. Together they had spent years transforming a dream into magnificent reality, only to witness it totally shattered in a few hundred seconds. The words that broke the silence surprised both of them:

"The back porch. That goddamned back porch!" cursed the husband. "It must have been all of that crap!"

It had suddenly occurred to him that the reason that they hadn't seen the gigantic ship approaching, was because their view astern was partially obstructed by all of the gear attached to the stern rail. This included propane tanks, fenders, an outboard engine, a wind generator, a horseshoe buoy, a barbecue, and so much other stuff that it reminded them of the comically cluttered back porch of the house that they had sold. But this wasn't funny. This was tragic. And it might prove deadly. Because for every miraculous liferaft survival story, who could know how many other such tiny, fragile craft had not made it?

Before they could ponder the severity of their situation for very long, their luck took a major turn for the better. The ship suddenly gave a long blast of its horn. A long, loud blast, which meant that she was still close. Then a powerful beam of light danced through their raft's bright orange canopy. It disappeared, came back, and then steadied itself on them. The ship was coming back and they would be rescued. This was truly amazing, for it was very likely that the huge vessel had barely even felt the impact.

Within an hour they had been hoisted aboard and were now seated in the captain's quarters. He was giving a heartfelt speech of apology. He admitted that he had no idea how it had happened and he seemed sincerely sorry. He promised to do his best with the shipping company's insurance agent to make certain that they received a just settlement. In his 27 years as a ship's officer, he had never experienced anything like this, and he was feeling deeply despondent.

So in a bizarre reversal of roles, the sailboat skipper felt obligated to cheer up the master of the ship that had just sunk his boat. He stood up, forgetting that he was still naked except for his foul-weather jacket, and began a short speech: "Thank you for your kind remarks and for the genuine remorse that you feel about this tragic accident. My wife and I are still probably in a state of shock, but we certainly realize that the most important thing is that we are alive. And hopefully you will feel a little better when you realize that all was not lost. Before our boat sank I was at least able to save this."

And then he reached into his pocket and with a grand flourish he triumphantly pulled out the Ziploc bag full of... *frozen peas.*

The Hurricane and the Poodle

I was single-handing down the south coast of the Forbidden Isle in total isolation. Since leaving Havana the previous month, I had not seen even one other foreign boat. Occasionally a local vessel would share an anchorage with me for a few hours, but at nightfall they would head off in search of either fish or the Gulf Stream to Miami.

The weather had been unsettled and unsettling. Wave after wave of muggy, squally depressions had been saturating southwest Cuba. I was particularly concerned because it was difficult for me to pick up the High Seas weather forecast on my inexpensive, battery-powered shortwave radio. Normally, if this happens, I can seek info from a fellow cruiser with a weatherfax onboard. But other sea gypsies were about as scarce as Linda Tripp photos in Monica Lewinsky's apartment.

All of these tropical waves were beginning to worry me since it was now prime hurricane season. So I decided to return to Key West, which seemed quite prudent because it had not been hit by a spinner in 76 years. But, as you can probably guess, that streak would end before it reached 77. It was probably appropriate that the first hurricane to plunder Key West in three-quarters of a century was male. And even though a name like Georges might not resonate with the intimidating malice of a Conan or Attila, it still packed a manly wallop. As for anyone who belittles 113 mph as being only a Category 2 storm, they can kiss my astrolabe. Fortunately my lithe little sloop *Aventura* escaped without a scratch. But we did have our usual disproportionate share of adventures. But before I share that saga with you I should describe the last disaster that my sailboat and I rode out together.

That was the 1989 earthquake in San Francisco. My boat was docked at Pier 39, only about 20 yards from one of the stages on which I performed. The magician who was entertaining there on that day had a reputation for being a bit unstable. And when one street performer, like me, refers to another such act as being somewhat marginal, that is really saying something. Suddenly, I heard a mass of people start screaming. Instantly I popped my head out of the hatch. I noticed that this guy's audience was not only hollering their heads off, but they were running away from the stage at decathalon speed. Wow, I thought, he must have finally snapped and decided to perform his 'Dance of the Corn Dog' routine for them.

But then windows started breaking in the shops on the pier and the water in the marina began gurgling with hula-hoop size bubbles. It was as if every hot tub in Marin County had been simultaneously turned on and piped over to us. Next the floating docks tried to levitate. They would lunge two feet up in the air and then crash down into the jacuzzi that used to be a marina. The docks, the pilings, and the water all seemed to be mad at each other. They were as out of control as many of the guests on the Jerry Springer Show.

At just about the time that I realized it was an earthquake, it was over. From the panoramic view of the city that was visible from my slip, it didn't appear too serious. But when I turned on my battery-powered radio, I got a very different opinion. It was time to switch into catastrophe mode. First, I drove to my sweetheart Hillary's apartment. It was OK, but she was a bit shaken. Next we checked my place and found some damage, but most importantly my lava lamp had survived. Hey, it's an original! Then we headed back to *Aventura*, since an ocean-going sailboat is a perfect self-sufficiency cocoon.

That night was extraordinary. The city was completely dark because of power outages. The only lights were the undulating peach glows from the fires still burning in some neighborhoods. The somber stillness was perforated only by helicopters and sirens. And then, amidst this Armageddon scene, an incredible moon arose. It was nearly full, and because of the dense smoke over Oakland, it had the color and velvet sheen of a blood-red rose.

Having now tangoed with both an earthquake and a hurricane, *Aventura* and I recommend that if you ever have a choice, take the quake. They're quick and there's no four-day paranoiac build-up. The aftermath, in terms of missing services and no water in showers, is about the same. Oh, and one more thing: in earthquakes, if you decide to play hero, it won't be in 80 or 90-knot winds.

Out of the 25 boats on my dock at the City Marina in Key West, only three of us rode out the 'cane onboard. It might be worth noting that we are all singlehanders, what one friend of mine calls 'the lunatic fringe of the cruising community.' The other boaters evacuated the Florida Keys or stayed ashore in secure buildings. These folks thought that I was nuts to stay aboard, but when they saw how many 20-ton trees fell onto houses in Key West, many of them changed their opinions. However, they didn't get to witness me at my nuttiest, or they would have agreed with the lunatic fringe assessment.

Every few minutes through the worst of the storm, I would poke my head out of the companionway hatch to make sure that *Aventura's* docklines weren't chafing. At the same time, I would squint through the horizontal spume and the flying Burger King signs to see if all of the other boats were OK. About three hours after the hurricane-force winds hit us, I noticed that a big center-cockpit sloop had come loose on the next dock over, and was threatening to destroy its neighbors.

Showtime! I called Larry and Mark on the radio and we launched our first Good Sailormaritan effort. Even going in, we considered each of these missions an 'Operation Stupido' because we were risking extreme bodily injury to save the property of some incompetent who had not secured his vessel properly. As we headed down the dock in our brightly colored foul-weather gear, hunched over and leaning heavily into the wind, we must have looked like three Quasimodos in search of a Mardi Gras parade.

Before we could get to the group of boats playing bumper sloops over on the next dock, the big one had dismasted the middle one, which was now threatening to topple the mast of the third one. Closer inspection revealed that the center one was getting slammed so hard that its hull-to-deck joint was already cracked open. It was getting the fiber kicked right out of its glass. We had to tame the big one quickly, but this was easier said than done since it meant we had to try to lasso a piling from about 12 feet away. In 80 knots of wind even a Grand National Rodeo roper probably would have failed.

But just as it appeared hopeless, Mark spotted a spring line that was still connected from a midship cleat to the piling. Now, calling this thing a line was an exaggeration of the highest magnitude. Michael Jordan's shoelaces are probably bigger and certainly stronger than this string was. However, it was our last resort. So we led it to a winch and Larry and I cranked it in. Slowly but unsurely, the big sloop inched over to the piling, and eventually we were able to get a real line around it. With this accomplished, the Three Quasimodos high-fived each other and savored the thrill of victory that only heroes and idiots can experience.

Our final rescue mission was of particular interest to me because it involved the boat right next to *Aventura*. It was a trawler that looked gigantic beside my svelte sloop. The size difference was so significant that it could have been a comparison illustration for 'with or without Viagra.' This boat had caught my attention the day before the hurricane because it was so ill prepared for what was coming. For one thing, unlike most of the other boats in the marina, it had only one set of docklines securing it. But what it lacked in this regard, it more than made up for in potential projectiles. On a railing behind the flying bridge were mounted an outboard engine, an anchor, and a barbecue. With wind from the wrong direction, any or all of these could become missiles of mayhem with lovely *Aventura* as their target.

Since the owners of the boat were out of the country, I secured the objectionable objects myself, and doubled up the lines on the side that jeopardized my boat. In the process of doing so, I made a most bizarre discovery. Outside the pilothouse was a welcome mat. However, it appeared that it was now being used as a cat box.

There wasn't any kitty litter sprinkled on it, but it could have definitely used some. I asked a neighbor if the local cats used the boat. He said that the debris actually came from a poodle that lived on the trawler. Naturally, I asked him why they hadn't cleaned up the mess before leaving. He just shook his head. So did I.

Later, during the storm, I heard what sounded like a shotgun blast next door and knew immediately that the trawler had snapped one of its lines. I popped my head out of the hatch to find out which way it was drifting, and was relieved to see, with the present wind angle, that it headed away from me toward the sailboat on the other side. I called the other two Quasimodos again and we humped into action. When Larry and Mark arrived to help me harness the beast, the hurricane was in a furious frenzy. The rain was as punishing as the shower in the Marquis de Sade's villa.

Larry jumped aboard. As he started up the defiled side deck, I shouted a warning, "Larry! Larry - not that way. Go the other way."

He halted and hollered back at me, "Why? What's wrong with this way?"

As the wind shrieked around us, I screamed as loudly as is humanly possible, "Poodle turds! POODLE TURDS!"

A confused look crossed his face as he bellowed back, "What? What did you say?"

"Poodle turds!" I screeched, "Poodle turds! I'll explain later!"

"Ray, you've finally lost it." came his barely audible reply.

The truth was that I had not lost it, but had instead found it. As I pointed out the welcome mat and its putrid offerings, the Three Quasimodos all paused and shared a spume-eating grin in 80 knots. For we had also found the most vital ingredient in surviving any major disaster - humor!

Tor Loves Thumper

With a name like Tor, the real world was out of the question. So he chose the sailing life. He liked the fact that not only was it the road less traveled; it was the road unseen. There were no highways to guide you across Mother Ocean. And as you glided over her, your wake simply disappeared - as though you had never been there. This suited Tor just fine. Because anyone named after the Viking god of thunder and lightning was more interested in making tracks than leaving tracks. All he wished was to wander the world's waters in search of adventure, romance, excitement, romance, mystery, and romance.

This yearning stemmed not only from his name, but also from his deepest DNA. On his dad's side, he was the son of an incurable risk-aholic. His father, Roy, chose the path less taken, or more accurately, the path hacked through the jungle with a machete. He did so because the Sky Bosun had shown him at a very early age how brief and fleeting life can be.

This occurred when Roy was just 17 years old. While walking down the street one day, he was frantically summoned to the nearby Turkish baths, where his dad had taken ill and collapsed. He arrived just in time to have his father die in his arms. Though just in his mid-teens, Tor's dad was wise enough to use this tragedy as an inspiration for his own future. He vowed to live with abandon and passion since he now knew with certitude that our allotted time here is so indiscernible.

His first great adventure was to answer an ad in a New York newspaper, seeking a photographer for an expedition to the unexplored headwaters of the Amazon. On the way to the interview he bought a camera at a pawnshop. Not only had he never used one before, he had never even held one before. But the pawnshop owner, when hearing of the boldness of his charade, was kind enough to teach him the basics.

Roy got the job. The expedition was more than just a success; it was a triumph. In those days photos were not downloaded via laptop and modem. Instead, they were transported by cannibal conga line and dugout canoes. For months he never knew whether the images even came out. Not only did they turn out black and white; they turned out golden, since they were circulated in newspapers all over the country. When he returned to New York, he had better than fame and fortune, he had fame and future. In fact he parlayed that expedition into a lifetime of photojournalism that would include dozens of books, hundreds of articles, innumerable magazine covers, and many prestigious photo and film awards. And to this day he still travels and treks with camera and laptop. His most recent journey was to the Galapagos Islands and Machu Picchu.

On his mom's side, Tor was the son of a daughter of a sailor. His grandfather Arnt's bio reads like it was written by Joseph Conrad. The son of a Norwegian boat builder, he shipped out of Oslo as a cabin boy in his second teen year aboard one of the planet's last working tall ships. Like many a Conrad character, he worked his way up to bosun and mate and finally master. When still just a cabin boy, he was aboard the three-masted barque *Sagitta* on her last voyage in the winter of 1916. Even though she was an unarmed merchant ship, she was torpedoed and sunk by a German submarine. As the survivors took to the lifeboats in the deadly frigid waters, the sub offered no assistance and stood off nearby, seeming to relish the agony of the doomed sailors.

Arnt was one of the four seamen in his open boat that survived. Fifteen did not. About half of them died by freezing. They were the lucky ones. The others, driven to madness by hunger, thirst, and cold, either threw themselves overboard or slit their own throats. After five days of Arctic cold, the lifeboat drifted onto the shore of a small fjord in Norway. A lone newsboy, on his early morning paper route, decided to take a shortcut that ran along the beach. It was a fortunate detour, because there he discovered the boat full of frozen, bloody bodies. Even though he presumed that they were all dead, he ran for help.

When the townspeople arrived they discovered that four of the sailors were still clinging to life - barely. They were the four youngest. Apparently they had just a little more life force coursing through their veins than did the others. Or maybe they had been the only ones who hadn't eaten the ship's dog when it had been butchered and devoured raw in the desperate deathboat.

Even though Tor was a few generations late for tall ships, his timing was perfect for small ships. When fiberglass boatbuilding proved successful, the cruising life became viable not just for wealthy 'yachtsmen' but for regular working people, and also for irregular, non-working hippies. Tor was practically a charter member of the Coconut Grove 'cruising without moving' fleet. But whereas most of his Miami neighbors chose their free anchorage for the cheap housing and constant parties, he was actually preparing for his seafaring life.

In 1978 he earned his U.S. Coast Guard Master's license. He then delivered boats from Florida to the Caribbean charter fleets. For years he was a captain in the Virgin Islands. He then began to mix selling boats with sailing them. He introduced the Cabo Rico line to the United States. He was Pacific Seacraft's first dealer in Fort Lauderdale. And today he is the exclusive New England broker for Valiant yachts. Over the years, 100,000 bluewater miles slid beneath his keel as he explored dozens of countries aboard the seven boats that he owned. He also sold numerous articles to sailing magazines in four different countries. But it all began with a humble boat and a humbling voyage.

Her name was *Thumper*. Although he hadn't asked the previous owner where the name came from, he presumed it was simply a description of the monstrous sound made by her ancient one-cylinder gasoline engine. Actually, he really didn't get to 'share a meaningful dialogue' with the man who was selling him the boat, since he seemed to be in a hurry. Apparently, he was also in a slightly guilty hurry. Because after the money was exchanged, and the papers were signed, and he was driving away, he suddenly stopped his car, walked back to Tor and handed him a paper bag. It contained a can of underwater epoxy putty and several dozen nails.

As soon as the travel lift returned *Thumper* to the water, the mystery of the strange gift was solved. Little geysers of water erupted at several spots and started to fill the bilge with considerable speed and enthusiasm. You see, Tor's new love was a converted lifeboat from a World War II Liberty ship. And she was made of steel, which was held together with rivets - a rapidly decreasing number of rivets. When the travel lift operator asked for an exorbitant price to lift the soggy little boat back onto land, Tor opted for the paper bag solution. It would not be the last time that he slavered underwater epoxy putty around a flathead nail, dove into the water, and pushed it into the hole that a rivet had recently abandoned.

Aside from the hull's propensity to transform itself into a colander, *Thumper* was a sweet and stout little boat. She had a mast that was thick enough to qualify as a telephone pole. Indeed, it was so sturdy that he could have carved 'Tor loves *Thumper*' into it without jeopardizing its strength. Her mainsail was gaff-rigged, and her jib was so patched that it looked like it had been attacked with a gaff. The forward part of the hull had been covered with plywood to create a little cabin. The rest of the ex-lifeboat was mostly open.

In the middle sat the beast that gave *Thumper* her name. Describing it as loud was polite understatement. In fact, some people upon first hearing it, were convinced that Tor was merrily manufacturing tractor parts in some sort of miniature, floating factory. Her upwind sailing performance left a bit to be desired. It probably had something to do with a hull shape that looked like it was modeled after a watermelon. But these lifeboats were not designed to be sailed, they were designed to be rescued.

Despite these minor deficiencies, there was no denying the fact that this little ship had character. Whether bobbing at anchor or promenading downwind, she exuded saltiness and bluewater bravado. And she was Tor's first love. So he took her on a honeymoon cruise. He single-handed her from Miami down the Florida

Keys. Because of her shallow draft, he was able to anchor in many little spots that even nowadays are usually uncrowded. Twenty-five years ago they were so empty that they were downright Darwinian.

After having studied all the proper books, this was his first actual experience at coastal piloting. As every pre-GPS navigator knows, it is a wondrous thrill finding your position on the planet by crossing lines of position, figuring set and drift, and monitoring a taffrail log. Tor delighted in learning that he was damned good at coastal and pretty good at celestial.

Key West was his first real port, and his top priority was no different from that of generations of sailors before him. However, his luck was far better than the great majority of his predecessors. You see, Tor didn't even have to go ashore to get… fortunate. Just after he got *Thumper's* anchor down near the little Simonton Street beach, he spotted the lovely Norma walking towards the water's edge in a most alluring bikini. He waved and smiled and she waved and smiled. He swam ashore and she swam back out to the boat with him. He left to continue his cruise a few days later and she left with him.

Now at this point it might be helpful to interject a bit more information about Tor's mother. Not only was *Thumper's* skipper blessed with high-octane 'adventure genes,' his tank was also full of 'handsome genes,' His mom, Doris, had been a very successful New York model. In fact, she was the gal who graced a million billboards and magazine ads in the Borden's campaign that also featured Elsie the Cow. So Tor could have also been named for the God of Hunks.

Thumper's next stop was in the beautiful Marquesas Keys about 30 miles from Key West. There, Norma and the captain of her heart frolicked in 'lagoon all to ourselves' mode. This reverie was ended by the arrival of two boats that were stopping briefly before continuing to the Dry Tortugas. Their enthusiastic descriptions of the strange, gigantic, isolated Fort Jefferson proved irresistible; so the three boats headed there the next day. Norma's long weekend was about to get longer, much longer.

The Dry Tortugas are a cluster of a half-dozen little islands that sit at the western end of the Florida Keys. Only one of these tiny sandspits is inhabited, and it is certainly no habitat for humanity. But it definitely qualifies as a habitat for humor. Because taking up 95 percent of the land on Garden Key is Fort Jefferson. Big Fort Jefferson. Gigantic Fort Jefferson! How big? Well, for about 100 years it was the largest brick structure in the Western Hemisphere.

Some brilliant naval strategist theorized that, since this is the 'corner' where shipping turns north up to Gulf Coast ports like New Orleans and Galveston, a fort positioned there could control the shipping lanes. However, in those days in the middle of the 19th century, a cannon only had a range of about three miles. So any ship wanting to circumvent this Gibraltar of the Americas only had to sail an extra mile off its rhumbline course to be safe.

If it was ridiculous from a strategic point of view, it was even more ludicrous from an engineering perspective. First, imagine transporting 16 million bricks, hundreds of cannons, and thousands of other items to this reef-strewn, hurricane-strafed wasteland, all by sailing ship. Once you get all of the equipment there, then the fun really begins. They didn't name these islands the Dry Tortugas because the turtles that nested there were teetotalers. They did so because there was no drinking water.

To solve this problem, the engineers built hundreds of cisterns under the fort. These concrete canteens could hold a million gallons of rainwater. Unfortunately, the coral beneath the fort could not hold up 16 million bricks. So the fort sank a few feet, thus cracking and ruining the cisterns. This was but one of a multitude of design blunders, which made one wonder if the project was handled by the Corps of Engineers or a Corps of Shriners.

Even though Fort Jefferson is bizarre, it is also beautiful. In the entire cruising world there is no other landfall quite like it. Nowhere else does such bold, rectangular redness rise from the waters to welcome a weary sea gypsy. For Tor and Norma it was a particularly memorable first sighting. They arrived late at night under a big moon, guided into the anchorage by the two boats that knew the channel. Veiled in the silver lunar lighting, the fort looked huge and mysterious. When they arose in the morning it looked huge and *red*. The long, amber rays of sunrise ricocheting off 16 million bricks will do that.

They spent their first day exploring the fort, fishing for their food, swimming, lazing under the coconut palms, snorkeling, reading, and visiting with other sailors. They passed their second and third days in similar 'relax to the max' fashion. On the fourth day they headed back to Key West. But before they could make many miles, the wind went from mild to malicious. So they headed back to Fort Shelter. That evening it turned into a full-force norther. This was quite unusual, since it was only mid-October, and such furious winds normally don't batter the Tortugas until late November.

Since it was so out of character, all of the sailors who were now pinned down in the anchorage were confident that it would blow itself out in a day or two. By about the seventh day their confidence was as feeble as the wind was fierce. Every day more boats arrived with tales of high winds, high waves, and high worries. The lucky ones made it in on their own. The less fortunate were towed in by the Coast Guard with broken masts and battered crews. Even the extremely seaworthy 100-foot schooner *Sea Star* had to hide behind the bricks.

Their food and water supplies were also low. So they sought assistance from the rangers. In those days the fort was a National Monument, administered by the U.S. Park Service. It had a large supply of both emergency water and military style C-rations. But it also had a head ranger whose middle name was apparently 'By the Book.' He was determined to release his emergency supplies only if he absolutely had to. When the crisis reached the two-week mark, he finally relented. Some sailors thought it was the sight of the Coast Guard helicopter airlifting an injured sailor out of the anchorage that softened his position. But Tor thought it was the Halloween party.

Even though everyone was weary of their situation, they made the best of it with a costume party on the beach. They sang and danced and laughed and even made up joke prizes for the best costumes. The top award was a Head Ranger Voodoo Doll with an ample supply of pins. Observing people having fun was apparently too much for him. He arrived unexpectedly in the middle of the party and announced that he would distribute food and water the next morning, but only if every vessel agreed to leave as soon as possible. Norma suspected that he was in the final stages of 'brickophobia.'

Two days later, the wind eased enough for the bigger boats to attempt an escape. By sundown, none had returned, which meant that conditions had moderated enough for them to continue. A major exodus took place the next day, and *Thumper* left at dawn on the day after that. It had been three weeks since they first dropped anchor beside the fort that rises from the sea.

The return sail was nerve-racking due to *Thumper*'s rivet-spitting tendencies. The anxiety was heightened by the fact that this was the first time that Tor had been out of sight of land with no buddy boats nearby. But skipper, mate, and vessel all made it back to Key West safely. And happily as well, for these were just the first of many miles that the three of them would share together.

And now, a quarter of a century later, as Tor sits in his yacht brokerage office, he probably wishes that he were sailing boats rather than selling boats. Perhaps he wonders what became of the sweet and stalwart Norma. And as he sends her his fond regards across the decades, he might just quietly laugh as he remembers their carefree days together, when it didn't matter if a three-day weekend turned into a three-week weekend.

Panama Canal Bumper Boats

When I told the cab driver that I was looking for a 'special hotel,' he smiled in an odd but enthusiastic way. He flashed a wide grin while simultaneously winking at me.

"Un poco amor?" he asked.

"No, I'm not looking for a little love," I responded.

"Mucho amor?" he then inquired, with a trace of admiration.

"No, I'm not looking for a lot of love, either," I replied.

"So what are you looking for?" he said in perfect English.

I was initially surprised by this abrupt switch in language until I reminded myself that I was in Panama, which had practically been an American occupation zone for the past century.

"I'm looking for a hotel where the backpackers stay," I said.

Apparently he didn't understand the word 'backpacker,' so I tried again. "A cheap hotel where the hippies stay,"

"Oh, you mean a *granola* hotel," he gleefully replied.

'Brilliant assessment,' I thought to myself, and then said, "Yes, exactly."

"No problema," he laughed. And off we went.

Now you might be wondering what I was seeking at a granola hotel. And if you knew that I was scheduled to transit the Panama Canal the very next day with my beautiful sloop *Aventura*, you'd really be curious about my strange mission. After all, shouldn't I be preparing my boat and crew for the trip through the canal? Well, since I'm a dyed-in-the-oilskin single-hander, I *had* no crew. Which is a major problem, because to pass through The Ditch you are practically required to bring along a committee. Not counting the skipper and the professional pilot, you need four people to handle the 125-foot ropes that connect the boat to the walls of the locks.

There are semi-professionals available, who hang around the yacht clubs at either end of the canal, who'll help you out - at $50 per day. But with the usual sailboat transit taking two days, using them would significantly dent my insignificant savings. So I was heading for the granolatel, hoping to find backpack travelers who would enjoy a free trip through the Panama Canal as line-handlers. My chances were good, because yogurt vagabonds are almost always open to unusual adventures, especially if free food, drink, and shelter are added to the equation. I should know; since I spent years out there on the third-class caravan myself.

Besides their affordability, these wanderers make excellent crew for other reasons. They are accustomed to traveling slowly, and they don't panic when confronted with the unexpected. As an added bonus, there was an excellent chance that I could assemble a polyglot crew. As a lifelong romantic, I've been in love with that phrase since first reading it in Melville or Conrad. So for years I've harbored a secret desire to see if I was man enough to skipper a polyglot crew. Rounding up volunteers wasn't difficult at all. In one quick trip to the Granola 6, I enlisted four people. They each hailed from a different country. I netted more nationalities than you'd find at a cab drivers' union hall.

There was Brigette, a young Canadian woman, and Bobby, her Costa Rican boyfriend. With his dreadlock hair and his 'no problem, mon' philosophy he was also an honorary Jamaican. Vanessa, a Brit, was full of vim, vigor, and cheerio helpfulness. And then there was 'zee beautiful Frenchwoman,' Simone. Her trip through the canal was symbolic of a more profound passage that she was making in her personal life. Both sloop and skipper were honored and delighted to be assisting her in both crossings.

We all assembled at the Balboa Yacht Club on the Pacific Ocean side on the night before departure. The place has a most convivial atmosphere since there is a singularity of purpose amongst the patrons. Nobody visits the BYC for its own sake. It is hardly a destination resort. Rather, it is a determination resort, one where everyone is solely dedicated to the pursuit of a new ocean for their boat. It is a sensible policy to assemble your crew of line-handlers the night before. That's because boats headed to the Atlantic usually leave at 0600 - or zero six rooster - as they say at the yacht club. If you are not on time, the fine is oceanic: $300.

Regardless of whether you're headed for the Atlantic or Pacific, the principle is the same. You start at sea level, ascend through a series of locks to what might be called hill level and then descend through another group of locks back down to sea level. Between those saltwater staircases are about 20 miles of lake and channel that must be traversed. If you are going to suffer any catastrophes, they will probably occur in the locks. Hundreds of sailboats make this crossing each year. For most of them the biggest problem is running out of ice cubes for sunset cocktails. But aboard *Aventura*, we had not just one, but two close calls.

The first occurred in the very first lock. We were rafted up to the starboard side of a 48-foot trawler-style powerboat. Another sailboat was attached to the trawler's port side. When motoring in a three-boat formation, the center vessel is usually in control. Being biggest and strongest it can easily maneuver the whole group. Each boat has a Panamanian advisor/pilot aboard to oversee things and issue instructions.

There are supposedly two critical times during the up-locking procedure. The first is when all the seawater is pumped into the lock, creating a gigantic hot-tub effect. However, imagine that it is Godzilla's jacuzzi and it is being filled through fire hose nozzles and not half-inch jets. The second crucial event is when the doors swing open and the huge ship in front of you that has been sharing the lock starts her propellers in order to move forward. This can instantly transform the chamber into a whitewater rafting test tank. With bad luck you can quickly go from outward bound to sideways bound. Most ship captains are very aware of the havoc that this can wreak on the miniature boats behind them, so they do it gently.

But since I had thoroughly prepared Team Polyglot for both of these calamities, something entirely different happened.

Because this is the uphill portion of the trip you enter at the bottom of the lock. Atop the walls are workers disguised as Lilliputians, who throw long, thin ropes down to you. These are then attached to your bigger diameter lines, which are hauled by hand back up to the top of the lock. The raft is now connected by four umbilical cords, which are each 125 feet long. As the water in the chamber rises, it is the line handlers' job to take up the slack so that the ropes don't wrap around rudders or propellers or rigging.

The initial positioning of the raft went perfectly. All of the lines were caught on the first attempt, passed across to the middle boat and secured properly. As my advisor instructed, I idled back my engine and put the transmission in neutral. The powerboat now had full control. Soon the huge gates astern of us closed and the water started churning in. During this awesome turbulence the skipper of the trawler was responsible for keeping us all in the center of the chamber using his powerful engine.

Whether it was from too much nervousness or too much non-chalance, I'll never know, but he lost control, big time! Naturally, it had to be in our direction. Instead of veering off to the left and jeopardizing the 40-foot sailboat, he careened to the right. My pilot calmly but firmly told me to put the boat back into gear, give the engine a strong burst of power and turn off to port.

Since *Aventura* weighs five tons and the other two boats weighed around 25 tons, I felt about as powerless as an average citizen trying to book a coach seat on Air Force One. The advisor from the middle boat, who had command of the entire raft, now superseded my pilot and hollered over to me to throw it into reverse and back down hard. I did exactly that, but there was no way that my little, 10 horsepower diesel could slow our crushing momentum.

Meanwhile, the skipper of the powerboat was feverishly manipulating his throttle and rudder controls. He was slamming the levers backwards and forwards with such ferocity that he looked like a backhoe operator with a boot full of fire ants.

Since I was now under the command of not just one but two advisors, I wasn't sure about my own right to give orders to my crew. But I was definitely sure that my beautiful sloop was in clear and present danger of being crushed between the wall and the other two boats. I felt like an egg on a pool table. It was just a matter of time - very little time. So I told the two line-handlers stationed near me to hurry forward and fend off. They moved to the bow obediently and swiftly, but unfortunately too quickly for me to tell them what 'fend off' meant.

But now I was saved by the courage and intelligence of Vanessa. The Jolly Brit had apparently been around boats long enough to understand the urgency of our emergency. She quickly sat on the bow pulpit, braced her back against the headstay wire and extended her legs so that her feet were against the canal wall. And then, pushing with all of her might, she kept us from being crushed and mangled.

Probably at this point the powerboat had regained control of the raft; but from my vantage point, this London lass straining on my bow looked as heroic as the legendary little Dutch boy with his finger in the dike. The advisor and I exchanged 'Can you believe that' looks.

The next two locks were approached with such extreme caution and concentration that we experienced no similar traumas. Once we began the long motoring stretch across Lake Gatun, I broke out some champagne to toast the Queen and her gallant British subject. I didn't care that it wasn't even 0900. The sun may not have been above the yardarm in Panama; but it was somewhere in Her Majesty's empire.

Our trip across the 20-mile lake was pleasantly uneventful. If a small boat does not arrive at the first lock on the Atlantic side by around 1530 they are instructed to anchor until the following morning. I pushed *Aventura's* little Volvo diesel pretty hard, and we thought we had made the deadline. That was because we could see the other two yachts from our earlier formation lining up to enter the lock. Our pilot radioed Canal Control asking permission for us to down-lock with them, but they rejected that request and instructed us to anchor nearby.

This was a bit discouraging, but it also had its good points. It meant that the Motley Polyglots and their frazzled skipper could relax with some festive rum drinks and a good meal. It was made doubly delightful because we were the only yacht anchored amidst 20 huge, handsome ships. For a sea gypsy like myself who considers a rust-bucket freighter more romantic than a candlelight dinner, this was heavenly.

The next morning, our new advisor was supposed to come aboard at 0930. When he hadn't arrived by 1130, I radioed Canal Control to ask if there was some scheduling change. The voice at CC checked his updated timetable and informed me that our pilot would be arriving at 1500 in the afternoon. I was a bit stunned by this long delay, so I asked politely if there was some supervisor that I could speak with in hopes that I could get it shortened. Apparently the voice from Control de Canal was in a bad mood. He launched into a tirade about how yachts transit at the convenience of the authorities, and how we cost them money, and how we are a damned nuisance. All of this is of course true. But the intensity of his outburst left the impression that his favorite daughter had run away with a visiting yachtsman.

The new advisor did not arrive until 1545 and we ended up entering the lock 40 minutes later than we could have on the previous day. The irony of this delay was not lost on me. Nor did I fail to notice the dramatic change in wind conditions. The prior afternoon had been dead locking calm, but today it was blowing 15 to 18 knots. Plus, it would be on our beam as we passed through the locks. Had we transited side-tied to a tugboat, as they had earlier told us we would be doing, the wind would not have been a factor due to the tug's strong engines. But at the last minute the tugboat was diverted elsewhere.

So now we would be down-locking in the center chamber. But we weren't entirely alone. Pulling in behind us was an 800-foot Chinese bulk carrier named *Joyous Society*. Our Panamanian advisor showed me on his computer printout that our lockmate was carrying a sizable amount of explosives. I silently hoped that her officers and crew also believed in joyous sobriety.

I first knew we might be in trouble when the pilot and I noticed that there were only three people stationed on the lock walls, ready to heave us four ropes. One person was missing from the starboard wall. However, the guy positioned there was large enough to equal two, perhaps two-and-a-half. Prior to seeing him, it had never occurred to me where Sumo wrestlers went after they retired from competition. Now I knew. But even though he was enormous, his size was exceeded by his slowness.

Since he was going to have to throw us two lines, it was important for him to be both quick and accurate. He was neither. His first toss fell a good 10 feet short of the boat. Rather than immediately heave us the other rope, he started retrieving the one that he had just thrown so badly. Our advisor radioed instructions over for him to toss the other line, but he ignored this plea.

What made this whole operation increasingly dangerous was the strong beam wind. Since maneuvering space in the locks is extremely limited, you can't motor at even close to full throttle or you will quickly run out of room. When up-locking you are down in this artificial canyon, and are shielded from the wind. But when down-locking you are completely at its mercy. By combining this beam wind and Señor Slowmo, the Sky Bosun had dealt me a very nasty hand.

My portside line-handlers were doing their best to get my 125-foot ropes secured on that side. But the wind was blowing the bow down to starboard. As instructed, I tried to gently but firmly power the boat to port. But with so much line in the water, there was a clear danger of getting one wrapped in the propeller. This would have dire consequences since it would lock up the engine and eliminate what little control we still had.

By this time, instead of being in the center of the chamber, we were halfway over to the right hand wall and drifting down fast. The good news was that we would soon be close enough for Senor Steppinfetchit to hand the lines over to us. The bad news was that the distance to the other wall was becoming so great that we were running out of rope.

With only about 10 feet of water between *Aventura* and the wall, and 10 seconds until impact, I told the advisor that I thought my only chance would be to give it full throttle and try to swing a counterclockwise U-turn. He radioed up to the portside wall, telling them to release my lines; and I hollered to the Polyglots to pull them in fast so that they wouldn't foul the prop. I put the tiller hard over, gave my little sloop a fistful of throttle and swung her around in a tight half circle. My concentration was so focused on not running into the side or front of the lock, or into any of the lines in the water, that I momentarily forgot about the huge ship that was approaching us from behind.

However, the canal folks provided me with a subtle reminder: sirens started going off and red emergency lights began flashing on the nearby walls. I nearly fouled my foulies! Then several loud-speakers started warning the workers that a ship carrying danger-ous explosives was entering the lock. To build dramatic tension even more, this dire message was delivered in Spanish and then repeated in English.

My alert pilot radioed the bridge of the *Joyous Society* and asked if they could stop long enough for us to dart out of the lock, swing a half circle and slip back in. They responded that they couldn't actually stop, because of their giga-ton momentum, but they would slow down as much as possible. Vanesssa yelled from the bow that all lines were clear up forward, and I could see them hauling in the last few feet of the stern line from my position at the tiller. Damn, this was gonna be close!

A boat-length after exiting the lock, I was swinging her back around to enter again. We were so close to the massive, unstoppable ship that the bulb on her bow looked touchable. It also appeared huge and red and menacing, like the nose of a drunk with a bad attitude. But we squeaked by it with minimum room and maximum heart rate.

I again turned my attention to the lock walls. On the port side two men were poised to throw us lines; and on the starboard side, Señor Sumo had now been joined by some other senor. The advisor breathed a sigh of relief. Mine came a minute later when all four ropes cascaded aboard *Aventura* and were snatched up by the Fabulous Polyglots. They tied them to my 125-foot lines, which were hauled over to the lock walls and quickly secured. On this second attempt the whole operation took less than two minutes and seemed effortless. Had the canal workers done their jobs properly, it could have gone that smoothly on the first try.

I was so drained by this ordeal, that instead of getting furious about the unnecessary jeopardy that my boat and crew had been subjected to, I simply rejoiced that we had prevailed over such bizarre adversity and emerged unscathed. However, such a fortunate escape certainly called for another round of festive rum drinks. Two minutes after docking at the Panama Canal Yacht Club, we let *Aventura* savor her new ocean in solitude while skipper and crew headed for the bar. As our glasses were hoisted, I called for a toast.

Bobby, the token male Polyglot, flashed a bright, Latin grin and said, "To the Panama Canal. Whoa, mon, The Ditch was a bitch."

"But she was also a beauty," said Simone in her lovely French accent.

"And we will certainly never forget her," added Brigette, from Canada.

"Nor will I ever forget my wonderful, polyglot crew," declared the grateful Yankee skipper.

"Ah, don't ya be getting mushy now!" teased Vanessa, our jolly Brit.

Kitty Wisdom

They decided to offer a reward for their cat. Not because he was lost, but because he was nameless. Choosing a boat name had been simple. Olivia and Jerry knew when they bought their cutter-rigged sailboat that she was no speedster. But her slow, gentle motion on the big ocean waves had pleased and comforted them. And so they named her *SloMo*.

Deciding on a name for their new kitten had been much more difficult. So they invited all of their neighbors from their Sausalito dock to a combination Christmas and cat-naming party. Whoever came up with the best name would win a bottle of champagne. The fact that the 'Christmas' bash took place in October only added to the festiveness of the event. But they had no choice in this regard, because by December they would be long gone on their cruise.

Their new kitten, which loved playing on the dock and in the nearby woods, had two prominent characteristics: he was all black except for two white spots on his head. One was on his nose and the other was directly above in the middle of his forehead.

Two hours into the eggnog, the kitty naming commenced. Olivia gave a short speech telling the guests that they were looking for a name that was original and clever.

"How about Blackie?" came the first suggestion.

"How about Spots?" came the second.

"Alright, knock it off, guys. This is semi-serious," said Jerry. "This little cat is probably going to travel all the way around the world. Few are the humans on this planet who achieve that, much less cats. So he deserves a worthy name. Also, something nautical would be nice."

"Well, he sure purrs like my new engine. So why don't you call him Yanmar?"

"That's better, but still not it," said Oli.

"Well, the two little spots look like stars. How about something celestial?"

"That's a possibility," said Jerry as he grabbed the Nautical Almanac to look for the navigational star index. Lots of exotic possibilities were found there, but because the young cat had two spots, they decided that a one star name wouldn't be sufficient. They tried combining the two shortest star names, but Enifvega seemed a bit too weird and esoteric even by San Francisco stan-dards.

Just when creative energy was beginning to wind down like a blender full of socks, someone said, "I've got it!"

She then picked up the kitty and started aiming him toward everyone as if he was a little, furry, toy boat.

"Can you see it?" she said.

But nobody could. Then she grabbed two of the tiny balls off the miniature Christmas tree. She placed a green one by the cat's right ear and a red one by his left. Again she aimed the toy furboat at all of the guests.

"Look, his spots are just like a big ship's mast and range lights," she said. "Let's name him Running Lights."

Bravos and applause greeted the clever idea, and the name was approved unanimously. Later, many people in the cruising fleet would shorten the name to its initials and call him R.L. But regardless of which name was used, he was soon one of the most beloved cats on the Seven Seas. He also became one of the most famous, because of an incident that occurred midway through *SloMo's* circumnavigation.

On a lovely calm night while crossing the Indian Ocean, Olivia was sitting in the cockpit petting Running Lights and admiring the full moon. She was reflecting on how subtly and yet profoundly the cruising life changes a person. The Man in the Moon was a perfect example of this. Way back in the beautiful little Mexican anchorage of Chacala, near Puerto Vallarta, some of the locals had shown her El Conejo en la Luna - The Rabbit in the Moon. Instead of seeing the face of a man, most Mexicans see the entire body of a rabbit facing sideways. It took Oli another cerveza and another ceviche to spot that image in the lunar contours, but now, a few years later, she always found herself greeting a full moon by whispering, "Hola, big rabbit."

In another hour she would awaken Jerry. But even though it was late in her watch, she wasn't feeling tired. Instead she was luxuriating in serene contentment. Her entire world seemed to be purring - the cat, the engine, the autopilot.

Suddenly there were some soft but sharp thwacks on the starboard sidedeck. Running Lights instantly went from a-purr to a-blur. There goes my little flying-fish commando, thought Olivia as she stood up to see how many had landed onboard. But the moonlit visitors were not flying fish. They were squid. She was quite familiar with them, but to R.L. they were both foreign and frightening. He quickly started back peddling, but he was losing traction on their goopy, slippery bodies. And then faster than you can say "calamari," Running Lights was overboard.

Oli threw the engine into neutral and hollered down into the cabin, "Jerry, Jerry! Wake up, wake up! Emergency!" She was disengaging the autopilot and starting to reverse course as Jerry bounded into the cockpit.

"What's wrong?"

"R.L. fell overboard."

"Was he wearing his emergency strobe light?"

"Not funny, Jer."

"Sorry, love. How long ago?"

"Only about 90 seconds."

"Well, that helps. A black cat in a black ocean is a bleak prospect. But we'll find him. Are you on a reciprocal course yet?"

"Just coming to it now."

"Alright. I'll get the searchlight."

But no little kitty appeared in the beam of the spotlight, and after 20 minutes their hopes were as dim as a winter sunrise in Alaska. They had backtracked, crisscrossed, circled - and Jerry had run out of ideas. But Olivia's female instincts came up with one last tactic.

"Jerry, turn off the spotlight and the engine. Let's try drifting. You know how well R.L. swims. We'll let him find us."

And miraculously, he did! In less than five minutes they spotted their beloved kitty's running lights headed towards them like a miniature freighter with whiskers at the bow and terror in its eyes.

And what a glorious sight that was.

After his night of water aerobics, Running Lights displayed no signs of aberrant behavior. That is to say, he remained as strange and inscrutable as any other cat.

Unlike many cruisers with grand and global aspirations, Oli, Jerry and R.L. actually completed a safe and splendid circumnavigation. Their friends back in Sausalito decided to throw them a party worthy of the accomplishment. And to make it even more memorable, they repeated the 'Christmas in October' theme. They also persuaded the current occupant of *SloMo's* slip to berth elsewhere for a few days so that Olivia, Jerry, and Running Lights could return to the exact spot from where they had begun their impressive voyage.

The congratulations and affection and eggnog flowed abundantly on that Indian summer Christmas Day. It was a reunion of special magnificence. After two hours of being admired and petted, the stalwart sea cat proved that he had never forgotten that traumatic night in the Indian Ocean. When none of the guests were watching, he went silently to the bow and surveyed the docks and woods that he remembered so well from his kitten days.

And then, with one last glance astern, he jumped lightly to the dock, ran down the pier, and disappeared into the woods. There he began a new life - a life where he would never have to swim again.

Gringo Loco

A rogue wave is not a pretty sight. And yet my memory of one such oncoming monster, as it towered above *Aventura*, is of over-powering and yet exquisite beauty. Its emerald-mountain majesty hurried my heart and stirred my sea-gypsy soul.

I was heading up the west coast of Mexico from Barra de Navidad to Puerto Vallarta. I was also heading uphill, or at least it seemed that way since both wind and current were pummeling my 30-foot sloop. Quite often, this passage can be moderate and manageable, but not his time. Apparently I had done something to really upset the Sky Bosun.

Perhaps it was my naughty entry in the sand-sculpture contest at Philomena's legendary St. Patrick's Day party for the cruising fleet in Melaque. Some of my competitors' beach creations were excellent, particularly the scuba diver riding on the back of the gigantic manta ray. But my masterpiece, like perhaps my entire outlook on life, was cut from a different coral.

It began with body molds of one of my favorite cruising couples, Reed and Cindy from the good sloop *Yobo*. He is a fallen-away lawyer who isn't a bit repentant. She is a former bartender who concocts keel-melting margaritas. I explained my skewed and lewd artistic vision to them and they immediately agreed to be the models. The contest began at 1300 and ended precisely at 1600. Timing was critical to our endeavor. I didn't want to bake my volunteers for hours on the beach; especially since Reed probably still remembered how to litigate.

So I waited until 1530, at which time I positioned them on their backs and began heaping on wet sand. Other cruisers had guessed that I was up to something strange, and a large crowd soon sur-rounded us. They good-naturedly tried to make my models laugh so that the hardening sand would crack. They gallantly offered to administer mouth-to-mouth resuscitation to Cindy. And they mercifully protected my subjects from dehydration by pouring unsolicited cervezas down their throats. All in all, these fun-loving sailor/spectators showed very little respect for an artist at work.

With only 10 minutes until deadline, it was time to perform my gender transplant. He was bequeathed a bosom so generous that he would never need a lifejacket again. She was provided a male protuberance of epic stature. It was accompanied by a handsome pair of manly satellites.

To me, this escapade seemed like good, semi-clean fun in the sun. But the judge was not amused. In fact, she was so distressed by my sculpture that she wouldn't even get near it. A local resident later told me that this young woman portrayed the Virgin Mary each year in the town's 'living nativity scene.' However, I wasn't invited to hang around until Christmas to verify this.

But perhaps the Sky Bosun was not mad at me because of my bawdy sand sculpture and was instead punishing me for breaking one of the cardinal rules of cruising: *Never have a tight deadline.* I rarely do, but this time it was unavoidable. Girlfriends who live in the Real World have much less flexibility in their work schedules than do single-handed sailors who have no work schedules. So if I was to rendezvous with my ladylove in La Paz for the Sea of Cortez Race Week, haste was unfortunately imperative.

The prevailing northwesterlies were stronger than usual that spring and this reinforced the adverse current. So, day after day it was bash, thrash, and smash to windward. Other cruisers, who were not constrained by time or the testosterone imperative, waited for more favorable conditions in the numerous protected anchorages along the coast. My only choice was which tack was less punishing. And this was no better than choosing between the Macarena and the Lambada.

I had covered about three-quarters of the distance between Barra and PV and was now about 12 miles from the narrow little harbor at Punta Ipala. That was the good news. The bad news was that I had been in approximately this same position for the last five hours. I knew this not just because of my GPS genie, but also because of the hilltop telecom tower that remained in the same relative position on a dozen inshore tacks.

The waves had now assumed sluggo shape, meaning every crest was positioned exactly a boatlength behind the previous one. My bow blasting into them threw back so much spray that it was like driving a convertible through a carwash. However, in their defense I should clarify that these waves were more tenacious and exhausting than terrifying. The spray was warm and as the sun began to set, it softened the angry scene, transforming it from malicious to gorgeous. After a while, the entire foaming, crashing maelstrom was glazed in twilight amber.

But suddenly, one nearby wave arched itself skyward with such determination that it looked like it wanted to fly. Backlit by the sun, it rose in translucent, emerald grandeur. I was transfixed by its cresting beauty until I realized that it was a *rogue*, that rare wave that can achieve boat-splintering height and power. And not only was it a liquid liquidator, but *Aventura* was headed right for it.

Before I could take any evasive action, I was skippering a submarine. I ducked under the dodger and clung to the mainsheet winch just before the wave thundered down on my fragile cocoon. But my stalwart sloop plunged right through the center of that wave and burst out of its back. I was amazed at how swiftly she purged all of that water from her cabin top and her decks. Aside from the cockpit well, which had attained aquarium depth, she seemed fine. The mast was still standing. There was no structural damage, and my VHF and GPS down below in the cabin were as dry as a buzzard's brunch.

Well, the Sky Bosun had dealt us a lickin' but we kept on tackin'. By 2200 that night we were approaching Punta Ipala. The shape of the hills behind this cove causes a fierce venturi effect, which accelerates the wind. So, to use an old sailor's term, it was 'honkin' as we tried to feel our way in with just starlight to guide us. I should also mention that this is the only harbor in all of Mexico where the cruising guide warns mariners of possible drug-smuggling operations. So in addition to darkness and exhaustion, I also had to be alert for blacked-out 'shrimp boats,' and the rat-a-tat-tat of semi-automatic weapons. I also had to dodge two cruising boats that were anchored in such a way that my only alternative was to drop my hook in very deep water.

I was beginning to wonder if there was anything right with this picture. Rocks off to port, breakers to starboard, too much wind, too little room and possible marijuana desperadoes. Naturally, as I tried to negotiate this Sailor's Nightmare Theme Park, the anchor did not set on the first try. So I had to haul in 185 feet of chain with my manual windlass. When my hefty anchor broke the surface, I was greeted by a wad of fishing net, line, and floats big enough to decorate an entire waterfront seafood restaurant. No wonder my trusty, oversized anchor didn't dig in.

I was so tired and testy that my implement of choice for removing all of that debris would have been a flame-thrower if I'd had one. Instead, I had to boat hook and hand hook that grunge garden onto my foredeck. It ended up completely filling a jumbo garbage bag. On the next attempt, the anchor set. I was now in deep water literally and otherwise. Because of the multitude of nearby dangers and the powerful wind still careening through the anchorage, I slept in the cockpit. My kitchen timer awoke me every 30 minutes so that I could ensure that we weren't dragging.

At 0200 the wind was still so strong that it seemed unlikely that I'd try rounding the dreaded Cabo Corrientes the next day. That was actually a relief because I was as drained as a fire extinguisher in a Pinto test lab. I needed a day's layover to regain my strength. But my abysmal luck held, and by 0300 the wind was dying. The accepted wisdom is that to round Corrientes northbound, one should leave Punta Ipala before dawn in order to cover the 12 miles to the cape before the wind goes from zephyr to banshee. By 0400 it had died completely, and I agonized over whether to try rounding in my depleted condition. I decided that the Sky Bosun was overdue to cut me some slack, and that with any luck I would be able to motor around this Cape of Currents by 0900. If it turned truly gruesome, I could blast back downwind to Ipala and try again the next day.

Anchor up, pedal down, and away we went. The wind was mild on the outside and the sea was lumpy but tolerable. After I had made it about six miles up the coast, a big, powerful ketch passed me doing about 9 knots. I recognized her silhouette as one of the two boats anchored nearby the night before. We established radio contact and wished each other good luck on the upcoming task.

An hour later he radioed back asking what my conditions were. My answer was that the wind was building quickly and the sea state was getting short and nasty, like a troll with a hangover. He told me to brace myself because he was now experiencing a steady 30 knots with miserable, steep, confused seas and swirling currents almost strong enough to produce whirlpools.

How could these mid-afternoon conditions already be assaulting us at 0700? Knowing that my window of opportunity for getting to Puerto Vallarta that day was closing quickly, I sheeted in the mainsail even harder and maxed out my engine. By 0800, the big ketch, helped by her long waterline and strong diesel, had rounded the cape. But with our short waterline and weak diesel the only thing we rounded was the Cape of No Hope. By 11 a.m., valiant little *Aventura* had been suffering and struggling for seven hours, expending every glass fiber of her being, trying to complete those 12 punishing miles. But by then we were just a plastic boat on a pathological sea.

Taunting us during this merciless struggle was the vulgar middle finger of the Cabo Corrientes lighthouse. For the last two hours we had been losing ground to it. At one point we were within three-quarters of a mile of it, but now the distance was a mile-and-a-half. With the wind stiffening and my will softening, it was time to admit defeat. I eased out the sails and headed back downwind towards Punta Ipala.

But then the Sky Bosun sucker punched me and really ticked

me off. He blew my cherished hat overboard. That battered, beloved hat had protected me from the melanoma monster for over 12,000 miles, and I wasn't about to let it go without a fight. It was anger up and helm down, as I began maneuvering to retrieve it. With both sails pulling, I made three passes but couldn't position the boat close enough. So I furled in the jib and tried motorsailing with only the main up. Still no success.

Next I dropped the mainsail and managed to motor right up beside my hat. I extended the boat hook to its full 10 feet. The hat was floating upside down with its chinstrap ready to serve as a perfect target. But as I reached for it, the other end of the boathook got tangled up in my nearby drink holder and my opportunity was quickly gone.

We circled back again. I stalled the boat out so that we would drift down to our floating grail. This time I took the boathook up onto the sidedeck to avoid interference. But as I made my lunge the sea parried with a puny wave just big enough to shove the hat up under the bow where I couldn't reach it. I was now furious and exhausted and beginning to truly lose it. All of the battering and stress of recent days had taken a terrible toll. I lay sprawled on the sidedeck with my head under the lifelines, staring blankly at the foaming, fuming water. And then a chilling, desperate clarity possessed me: *I must get that hat!*

When I returned to the cockpit, all of my senses seemed suddenly heightened and attuned. The tiller felt like a wizard's staff in my hand. The scream of the wind was somehow mystically silenced. My sloop seemed to be gliding in ultra-slow motion as she bore down on the hat. When the moment arrived, I looked over the transom to make sure that the stern steps were down. Then I unhooked the tether on my harness. And finally, at the precise moment that I stalled out the boat alongside the hat, I dropped overboard.

Perfect timing. With my left hand I snatched the hat, with my right hand I grabbed the self-steering vane and reconnected to my boat. I put the chinstrap in my teeth and with both hands free I quickly clambered up the steps and back into the cockpit. Triumphantly I placed the dripping hat on my head and tightly cinched the chinstrap. This was one of those exalted moments in life to be savored and stored away as good medicine for bad times. But I didn't get to relish it for long; because seconds later I heard a gunshot.

It jolted me off my seat and pivoted me around toward the lighthouse where I saw the trail of an orange smoke flare descending into the sea. I reached into the cabin and grabbed my binoculars. I focused them on a figure standing at the lighthouse wall and was then treated to one of the most memorable sights of my life. The lighthouse keeper, seeing through his field glasses that I was now looking at him, put down the flare pistol and binoculars, raised his hands above his head and... *began applauding!*

I was profoundly touched by this playful but respectful gesture. For although I am a sailor, I am also a Teller of Tales. And in Mexico, television has not yet completely eliminated the spinning of yarns. So someday, when I am alone, battling a frenzied, uncaring ocean, I will find courage and strength knowing that the lighthouse keeper of Cabo Corrientes is passing along my story, the tale of the gringo loco who jumped overboard to rescue a cheap, beat-up straw hat.

A Sailor and his Donkey

Leah nudged me with her foot and whispered, "Check out the banana hammock!"

"The what?" came my innocent reply.

"The banana hammock!" she repeated with mounting enthusiasm. "Can't you see his Speedos yet? They're even smaller than yours and they're bright yellow."

As I finished rowing my dinghy up to their Peterson 44, I got my first glimpse of his impressive fruit of the loom. My gaze then traveled up to his well-tanned face. It was bordered by a blonde beard, which framed a Cheshire-cat grin as bright as his tiny, yellow swimtrunks.

"Come aboard," his wife hollered down to us. "We don't have a ladder, so just grab ahold of anything and pull yourselves up."

Leah grabbed a stanchion, and hoisted her long, lithe body up onto their boat. I followed, and we were soon sipping wine coolers with our new friends, Sandy and Andie. These drinks were most appropriate, because our hosts were such enthusiastic wine lovers that they had named their boat *The Merlot Mermaid* in honor of their favorite red.

The effervescence of the wine spritzers was a perfect match for their easygoing philosophy. Even by sea-gypsy standards, their approach toward life in general, and cruising in particular, was relaxed and refreshing. This ability to go with the flow was clearly demonstrated as we sipped our wine cooler and they realized that they weren't even in the right harbor.

I had deliberately chosen this 'outside' anchorage at Tenacatita, on Mexico's Pacific coast, because it is usually empty, whereas the 'inside' one is normally crowded. This was Leah's first cruise aboard *Aventura*, following our meeting at the notorious Valentine's Day potluck party in Barra de Navidad. 'Outercatita,' as I liked to call it, was to be our little hideaway, where we could enjoy plenty of moonlit privacy. So when I turned into this seldom-used bay, I was surprised to see this big cutter follow us in. I had expected them to head for the normal inside anchorage. And, in fact, that's where they meant to go. Their navigation was just a few miles west of accurate.

When they learned of their mistake as we sat sipping our drinks, they reacted with neither the surprise nor the embarrass-ment that one might expect. Instead, Andie said, "Well, that's no big deal. We haven't found any other anchorage on the first try either." Upon hearing this, Sandy didn't get the least bit defensive about his navigational prowess. He just took another sip of his merlot cooler and chased it with one of his wide, sparkling grins. Surely, I mused, this was one couple who had mastered the art of accepting themselves as they are. The next story that I heard about them a few months later confirmed this assessment.

On the way from Golfito, Costa Rica, to Panama, *The Merlot Mermaid* did something quite strange. They anchored off Punta Burica, which marks the border between these two countries. This was unusual because the water at that location is so shallow that even a mile from land it is only about 20 feet deep. Thus, you have to anchor far from shore where there is little protection from the wind. And as with any big cape, the currents are confused and bizarre - sort of like an octopus trying to do the Macarena.

This became all too apparent about 30 minutes before sunset when the current turned them beam-on to the wind, making the *Mermaid's* motion very uncomfortable. Sandy decided to remedy the situation by setting a stern anchor with the dinghy. He chose not to use the outboard motor because it was mounted on the aft rail, and would have to be lowered and attached to the dinghy. Such an operation would significantly reduce the time that he and Andie could spend savoring the merlot sunset. Besides, after rowing out the anchor and dropping it from the inflatable, he could simply pull himself back to the mothership along the anchor rope.

Meanwhile, the Sky Bosun was apparently observing all of this while enjoying a wine cooler himself. And it occurred to him that this simple operation would be a lot more entertaining if something went wrong; or if a whole bunch of somethings went wrong. And so it came to pass...

First, when Sandy dropped the anchor, the line attached to it slithered out of the dinghy in rapid pursuit of its heavier companion. Before you could say, 'A smokey nose with just a touch of fruitiness and a hint of the oak barrel,' the anchor, chain and rope were all at the bottom of the sea. Sandy just grinned. Then he reached for the oars and began to dispel the myth that Cheshire cats can't row. Smoothly and steadily he covered half of the distance back to his wife. But suddenly one of the oars broke in half at the joint and the important part drifted away.

Sandy now started paddling with the one remaining oar, but his valiant efforts only produced motion that went sideways, backward, and around in circles. From their underwater perspective, the nearby fish must have been watching the gyrating dinghy and thinking to themselves, 'Could this be the Lambada, the Forbidden Dance of Love?'

A half-hour passed and whole darkness descended. Sandy realized that he wasn't going to make it back to the boat, so he began trying to steer the dinghy where he thought land was. This was an excellent strategy because if the westward-setting current grabbed hold of the dinghy, the next land he encountered might very well be Guam.

Fortunately, the stars were bright enough to dimly outline the spine of Punta Burica and eventually he landed there on the beach. Because the cable lock for his dinghy was attached to the outboard, he decided to do the prudent thing and hide the dink behind some bushes. Little did he realize that there were so few humans in the vicinity, that it was not even slightly in jeopardy. The only way it would get stolen was if a barracuda made an evolutionary leap and walked up the beach to abscond with it.

Next, Sandy started walking up the coast to search for help. Whether our barefoot boy was actually whistling we don't really know, but you could certainly wager that he was grinning. That's because this escapade had now gone from a silly mishap to a bonafide adventure. After walking a short distance, he noticed that he was getting slightly chilled, and he remembered that Andie had thrown a lifejacket into the dinghy just before he rowed away. So he went back and fetched it. If he did find anybody on this remote peninsula, he would certainly make a bold fashion statement in his vivid yellow speedos and his lifejacket that was orange enough to induce permanent retina damage.

He soon spotted a light coming from a small cabin in a clearing. He could faintly hear voices. So he hitched up his 'trousers,' adjusted his 'jacket' and walked up to the doorway of the rustic hut. The impact of his arrival was overwhelming. Had Madonna herself appeared wearing a chiffon gown and singing, 'Don't cry for me, Punta Burica,' the inhabitants could not have been more stunned. All jaws dropped. All conversation stopped. Obviously this visitor was bizarre, but they didn't know yet whether he was also dangerous. Then he grinned, and the tension was broken. For, surely, anybody with a shrimp- eating grin like that had to be harmless.

Sensing some urgency and purpose to his unexpected visit, they invited him in where he sat down on a chair that smelled distinctly 'fishy.' Or was it the table that smelled so pungent? Or perhaps the entire cabin? he wondered. From this clue he deduced that they probably did not make their living designing websites on the Internet, but instead were humble fisherfolk.

Communication now became an interesting game. Sandy's knowledge of Spanish was limited to the words *hola, vino,* and *dinero.* No matter how hard he tried; he couldn't find a way of arranging these words to convey, "Hello, could you give me a ride back to my boat, which is anchored nearby. My wife, who is probably terrified about now, would really appreciate the help and we would reward you handsomely."

But efforts at conversation were moving forward. An old man kept saying, "Ron." Did this mean that this grandfather guy was named Ron? Or did the old timer think that Sandy was named Ron? It was very confusing. Actually, it was even more confusing than he realized, because ron is the Spanish word for rum. The grandfather was asking Sandy if he wanted some. Eventually, the woman who seemed to be the mother of the household, by-passed this verbal roadblock by placing a glass of rum in front of Sandy and saying emphatically, "Ron."

Finally he got it.

And he drank it.

This had a pronounced warming and loosening effect on both his body and his mind. So now he began to pantomime his predicament to them. He made gestures to indicate sailing, anchoring, a broken oar, and a worried wife. But even though his flailing arms and wild facial expressions made absolutely no sense to them, they hospitably concealed this with smiles and nods.

But eventually, with a little more ron, some crayons borrowed from the two children, and some very fishy-smelling paper, Sandy was able to convey that he needed a lift back to his boat. And sure enough these fisherfolk had a nice 20-foot panga with a big, strong outboard. The bad news was that the father of the household was out fishing in it, and wouldn't return until the middle of the next day.

Sandy might have been willing to resign himself to this rather long wait, but the Sky Bosun, seeking additional entertainment, decided to spin the situation in an entirely different direction. Suddenly the grandfather said, "Burro!" And then the mother also exclaimed, "Burro!" Now the kids joined in and all four of them were circling the table chanting, "Burro, Burro!"

Our scantily clad hero certainly knew what burro meant, but he definitely didn't know how it applied to this situation. He also didn't know what kind of strange fetishes these people who lived such an isolated existence might have. Sitting there in his miniscule yellow speedos, he suddenly felt vulnerable and a bit worried.

Meanwhile, aboard *The Merlot Mermaid*, Andie had managed to radio some other cruisers back in Golfito, who in turn notified the Costa Rican Coast Guard. About the time that the Coasties arrived, a pretty stiff breeze picked up. This put the lovely cutter in jeopardy, since now she was off a lee shore with a rising wind. The one rescue officer, who spoke English, suggested that they shift the *Mermaid* around to the other side of the peninsula.

After completing this move, they began searching for Sandy. They cruised up and down the length of the beach shining a powerful spotlight along the shore, but they didn't find him. What was perhaps even more disturbing was the fact that they didn't find the dinghy either.

Andie's frightened imagination went wild. Had he gotten swept out to sea? Would it take an air search to find him? Then it went wilder. Weren't these shark-infested waters? Could he have become the Catch of the Day? Eventually, it went wildest. What if this remote peninsula was home to a tribe of banana worshippers, whose legends foretold of the arrival of a yellow-haired Banana God? And might all of the tribe's maidens be lined up at this very moment to test Sandy's 'godliness?'

Actually, at that moment, Sandy wasn't feeling very godlike. But he certainly felt like some kind of weird king in a mistaken-identity novel. That's because he was now riding a donkey that was being led up a mountain trail by three generations of fisherfolk in the middle of the night. The absurdity of the scene was highlighted by his yellow speedos and orange lifejacket.

At some point during their cross-cultural communication, the little family had realized that they had a cousin with a boat who probably wasn't out fishing that night because his wife was due to have a baby. The problem was that they lived on the other side of the mountain. Actually, the real problem was the visitor's lack of shoes. None of theirs would fit him, and he couldn't traipse that mountain trail barefoot in the middle of the night. That's when the grandfather had hit upon the idea of transporting him on the family donkey.

Shortly before dawn, this Fellini-esque procession arrived at the hut of their cousin. If Sandy's previous apparition had been mind-boggling, imagine how much more bizarre it was with him riding a donkey while wearing his Miami Beach gigolo outfit. Talk about artificially inducing labor! Initially, the husband and wife tried to go back to sleep, since obviously they must be having some weird dream. But then they wondered how they both could be having the exact same weird dream. Their cousins, who were by now used to Sandy's eccentric threads, found this immensely amusing.

After all the laughter had subsided, there was a lively debate concerning who would escort Sandy and the cousin in the boat. Everyone wanted to go; for certainly such an outlandish visitation would never again occur at lonely Punta Burica. Eventually the grandfather won out because he had thought of the burro idea, and because it would be best if the mother stayed with the pregnant wife. So off they went.

Since it was now dawn, it should have been easy to find the one sailboat anchored off this isolated point. That is, if there *was* one anchored there. Currently, there was one bobbing *behind* Punta Burica, but Sandy didn't know that. So even if he could speak Spanish like Julio Iglesias, he would have still had a tough time explaining this significant discrepancy in his tale of woe.

While Sandy pondered his options, the grandfather and cousin were trying to fathom the true depths of this gringo's looniness. Could he actually be dangerous? Did he want to steal their boat? Was that a gun in his speedos? Just as their paranoia was beginning to crest, Sandy disarmed them with his secret weapon. He unleashed one of his widest, stupidest grins. This comforted them enormously. Almost as much as the news that was about to be delivered to them from the Coast Guard boat which had just rounded the point and was speeding their way.

Minutes later there was a joyous reunion between Andie and Sandy. Then everyone spent 10 minutes and two languages describing all of the strange events of the last 12 hours. To top off this boisterous conversation, Andie ceremoniously reached into her satchel and said to her husband, "Sandy, I knew that you would be hungry when we found you, so I brought this along."

Then she tenderly presented him a big, ripe, yellow banana. And as a delighted grin brightened his face, it was mirrored by the happy smiles of the entire group as they sat bobbing in their boats where Costa Rica and Panama meet the sea.

Operation Cream of Mushroom

Sailors who singlehand little boats across big oceans learn many lessons. Some of these are deeply profound, but for unknown reasons, mine tend to be more comic than cosmic. Perhaps you might be interested in one humorous example of this arcane knowledge that has made my cruising a lot less aggravating and a lot more entertaining.

My stalwart 30-footer is among that elite group of offshore sloops that has achieved the United States Coast Guard 'safety inspection' trifecta. By this I mean that *Aventura* has been boarded and examined in a Bay (San Francisco), a Gulf (Panama) and a Sea (Caribbean).

Occasionally I have discussed this 'Coastie-magnet' phenomenon with other sailors while we replenished at various palm-shaded fuel docks. (Hey, just because it is served from a blender instead of a pump, doesn't mean it isn't a type of fuel!) Some of these fellow sea gypsies have suggested that because of the increasing number of women in the Coast Guard, perhaps it's my good looks that are attracting so much attention.

My response to such a generous theory is that it could only result from the failure of their eyesight or the success of the bartender. I do appreciate their kindness in the face of such contrary evidence, but it seems about as accurate as a Florida vote count. Whereas I might have once been described as molten, the appropriate adjective today is probably molting. But back to the story. I should hereby emphasize that my intent is not to whine about the frequency of these governmental courtesy calls, but to share with you my tactic for shortening their duration.

Aventura and I were beating against the trade winds, trying to lay the Cayman Islands. My friends aboard the big, blue ketch *Starship* had enticed me there for a visit. They claimed that it was a great place for an aberrant sailor like myself, who packs his bilge full of bowling balls.

So David and Nan, the respective Captain and Admiral of *Starship*, thought that I could fluff up the ol' cruising kitty by performing at one of the comedy clubs on Grand Cayman. They figured that my off-the-ball humor might appeal to islanders and visitors alike (although discerning intellects might interject that there are few things in the world that are less alike than locals and tourists).

Anyway, here I was, after five days of tough windward sailing up from Isla San Andreas; or, as I like to call it, Isla San Sobering. This pleasant little spot is a stark reminder that The Seven Seas are often The Severe Seas. The reefs and shallows that surround this handsome island are practically gridlocked with shipwrecks. And these are not just funky, little inter-island freighters; these are *big* ships. Presumably, they were outfitted with plenty of electronic navigation equipment. So any yachtsman with unswerving faith in their GPS and radar, should swerve by Isla San Andreas for a reality refresher.

But Isla San Sobering was now five days astern and Grand Cayman was less than one day ahead. Even though the conditions were particularly sloppy, I was feeling that special joy of impending landfall that is reserved only for singlehanded oceaneers. Indeed, I was so imperturbably mellow that even the sight of a huge guided-missile cruiser approaching at 'all ahead full' did not phase me. However, when it proceeded to steer a complete circle around *Aventura*, I suspected that we were not just ships passing in the noon.

The tightness and speed of the 360 that this enormous vessel executed around my humbled sailboat was awe-inspiring. Since she had a distinctive pale lime tint to her combat coloring, I guessed that she was in Her Majesty's Service. This was reassuring since it meant that I could just enjoy this display of donutry without worrying about being boarded for another 'safety inspection.'

Ha! Maybe in a perfect world, but not in my world. Suddenly an officer from *HMS Southampton* was hailing me on the VHF radio in a dashing British accent. He was instructing me to heave to and prepare for a... safety inspection. What was this? "Son of a bush!" I cursed with prophetic accuracy. Was *Aventura* suddenly looking so unseaworthy that every navy on the planet felt obliged to examine her? Damn, I always did my best to keep her shipshape and Bristol fashion, as my new neighbors might describe it. And this is no slight task for a solo sea rover who also tries to honor his bachelor responsibilities.

But the mystery was revealed before *Aventura's* skipper could become unraveled. The Southampton was hosting a U.S. Coast Guard contingent. I can't recall whether the actual term 'drug interdiction unit' was used, but it wouldn't take a cartel of Einsteins to arrive at this conclusion.

Before I could sarcastically ask the huge cruiser on which side to position my fenders for our impending raft-up, they started lowering a center-console inflatable. This was a very impressive looking tender that would have pleased the oily heart of any OPEC owner of a Monte Carlo megayacht. Through my binoculars I also noted that the British bosuns aboard the dinghy looked ruddy and salty, but the complexions of the Coasties were turning a pale green, quite similar to the color of the warship's hull.

This was a perfect time to launch Operation COMS - Cream Of Mushroom Soup. I sped below and opened a can of Campbell's finest, and plopped it in a saucepan. I stirred it until it attained the perfect degree of lumpiness, poured in some soy sauce for enhanced rancid coloring, and then added the crowning touch, a couple of rotten egg yolks that are kept handy in a Tupperware jar, just for this purpose. After stirring everything together, it was indisputable that here was a recipe that had 'hurl' written all over it.

Next I went topside and complied with my orders to heave to. I must admit to doing so with malice aforethought. Heaving to normally dampens the rolling of a boat, but by adjusting the mainsail, tiller, and backed jib just so, one can actually accentuate the boat's motion and make it particularly sloppy and jerky.

Since the Sky Bosun had blessed me with a constitution that never gets seasick, such movement would not bother me. But my guess was that it would seriously distress my approaching inspectors. When the inflatable pulled alongside, the Coast Guard lads were already sporting such pale green complexions that they looked like a trio of albino aliens.

Before helping them aboard, the two Brits handed me a six-pack of some fine English beer. Sailors in the Royal Navy still receive a daily ration of ale and rum. (Draft boards - they don't need no stinking draft boards!) I thanked them sincerely for this generosity. My suspicion was that it was a small gesture to compensate for the absurdity of this search. After all, would I possibly risk my magnificent, little *Aventura* for the puny profits that could be made from smuggling? My boat is so small that even a half a ton of marijuana stowed below would overwhelm the interior so completely that she would look like a floating compost heap.

Once the boarding party was in the cockpit, I welcomed them with, "Sorry about the way that my boat jumps around, but that's the nature of little 30-foot, 5-ton sloops. Actually, this is pleasant compared with the cabin where everything is sort of wet and clammy and smelly and claustrophobic. So, shall we go below?"

"Why don't I stay up here and begin the paperwork?" said the greenest of the three.

"Great idea," I replied, "would you like me to hand you up my passport and boat documents?"

"Thanks," he said, in a voice that was half relief and half gargle.

Down below the other two commenced a thorough and professional inspection - that is to say one grabbed the handle at the chart table and sort of looked around while the other clung to my mast and sort of looked around. Mostly there were staring out the portholes towards the horizon in an effort to still the demons that were playing foosball with their inner ears.

Sensing their vulnerability and not wanting to prolong their misery, I suggested that they might want to check the bilge. As they both knelt down to lift the bilge board, I applied the Cream of

Mushroom terminator. Having firmly put the lid on this cruel gruel, it had now been fermenting for several minutes.

With a flourish of hospitality, I removed the lid and asked them if they would care for some soup. Then I placed the pan directly in front of their eyes and noses. Even for me who was expecting it, this was a staggering development. The appearance and stench of the concoction was Vile with a capital V! It looked and smelled like the pot that the pelican puked in.

My jolted guests lunged up the companionway ladder faster than Regis Philbin scurrying to a photo op. As they sat in the cockpit swallowing big gulps of soothing sea air, they asked their cohort if he was almost finished with the paperwork. Thankfully for their sake, he said yes. They all piled into the inflatable and sped back to the massive stability of the British cruiser. Their entire visit had taken less than five minutes.

As they went bounding over the lumpy seas, I looked at the paperwork that they had handed me and noticed that upon my arrival in Miami I must report to the Coast Guard and demonstrate that I had rectified the reason that *Aventura* had failed her safety inspection. And just what was my offense? Having no horseshoe buoy.

For the remainder of my sail to the Cayman Islands, I tried to solve the riddle of just who might throw me that life ring if I did fall overboard. Ah, the inscrutable mysteries of the sea!

The Petrified Chapel

This ghost town was different. It wasn't in the California foothills, it was beside the Sea of Cortez. It wasn't from the last century, it was from the last decade. And it also wasn't on the normal Baja cruisers' route. But sure as there is salt in the sea, it was worth a visit.

Bahia Salinas had been its name and salt had been its game. Enormous evaporation ponds covered the valley floor astern of the beachfront town. Several years after operations had ceased, the salt flats were intact, giving the otherwise jumbled terrain an eerie, rectangular symmetry. The site is located on the eastern side of Isla Carmen, which is about 10 miles from Loreto on the Baja Peninsula. The bay is shunned by many sailors for two main reasons: it is very shallow, and it is very open to the south.

On my approach, *Aventura* was already in 14 feet of water

nearly a mile from shore. I dropped the anchor in 11 feet and the shoaling was so gradual that I was still more than 100 yards from the beach. Looking south, the second difficulty with this spot was quite apparent. It is very exposed. The fetch is endless, seemingly stretching all the way to Ecuador. Which means that some mighty wicked waves could build up and jeopardize one's boat.

It should be mentioned that this intriguing locale can also be reached by trekking overland from the popular Puerto Ballandra anchorage on the western side of Isla Carmen. However, the hike is on a rough and poorly marked trail across mountain, desert, and salt flat. Personally, I wouldn't attempt it without the help of the Lost Tribe of Baja Sherpas.

Beaching my dinghy, I was glad that I don't use an outboard, because my oars came in handy in fending off my welcoming committee of four wild dogs. They may have been domesticated pets at one stage of their doghood, but in their current condition they could have been the poster pups for the concept of 'lean and mean.' But like all wise and wily cruisers, I had come ashore bearing gifts for possible barter.

A month earlier, a sailor friend had achieved the ultimate trade with some Mexican fishermen when he had exchanged their lobster for his Spam. This triumph of commerce inspired me to always include a can of Spam in my go-ashore kit. Thus, I wadded up a glob of the 'substance' for each of the teeth-baring dogs. This proved to be the perfect sedative for them. So, already this out-of-the-way stop had been worthwhile, since I had finally discovered an actual use for Spam - as a suppressant for crazed, feral dogs residing in salt-mine ghost towns. The canines and I now headed off to explore the town.

Scattered and shattered along the water's edge were a couple of small tugboats and a few diminutive salt barges. It was difficult to determine whether these vessels had been deliberately beached or whether they had broken free of their moorings. Regardless, they were a trespasser's dream. Inshore, the town is bisected by a sizable pier that apparently piped salt to the lighters, which transported it to the bigger ships anchored farther out in the bay. On one side of this pier are the industrial and administrative buildings, and on the other are the houses, school, and chapel.

It didn't take a Señor Holmes to discover that everything had been ransacked. Not just the engines from the generators or the tires from the tractors, but doorknobs, faucets, and light sockets from all of the buildings. If an object could be of value back in Baja, and if it was removable, it had been liberated. This redistribution of wealth made perfect sense to me. In a struggling economy like Baja's, why leave goods and hardware on a deserted island, when there were so many destitute people 10 miles across the water?

Like many human tourists, my canine escorts lost their enthusiasm before the end of our junket. Our amble through the shambles abruptly ended at the moment that I reached for the chapel doorknob and began to open the door. They started barking madly, and ran off toward the beach, looking for all the world as if they were being chased by the mythical Salt Leopard.

Their abrupt retreat was the first clue that there was something strange about this building. The second clue was the fact that there was even a doorknob to turn. This was cause for a pause. So I stepped backward and surveyed the little chapel more carefully. Hmm. None of the windows was broken, the doors were on their hinges, and even the valuable bronze bell was in its niche at the peak of the roof. Could it be that the religious fervor of these simple people had been so strong that it protected this tiny church from the fate that had befallen the rest of the plundered town?

The answer was dramatically revealed as I opened the door. Everything was completely intact - the pews, altar, stations of the cross - everything. Nothing had been stolen, broken or destroyed. On the altar there was even a mimeographed copy of Holy Week services that had been scheduled for the final days of the town's existence.

Standing there in the stained-glass light, I could sense an awe-inspiring feeling of devotion and sanctity in this dusty, deserted chapel that could not be surpassed in even the mightiest of cathedrals. Then I thought to myself that perhaps somewhere in the heavenly realm there is a mothball fleet of abandoned churches. And if so, this humble chapel at Bahia Salinas should be its flagship.

Once Is Enough!

This story will sound suspiciously like a bad joke, but it isn't funny if your name is Peter Augusto, and you barely survived to tell the tale. Even before the voyage that I am about to describe, Peter was already an endangered species. That's because he is a true, bluewater man in a cruising world increasingly populated by daylight, night-fright sailors who would probably rather motor.

Peter had recently done a long, oceanic loop of the Atlantic from North Carolina to Bermuda, the Azores, the Cape Verdes, Brazil, the Caribbean and back to the Carolinas. This tale occurred during his next passage from North Carolina directly to the Virgin Islands. Sailing 'down island' seemed like a perfect way to inaugurate the new millennium, so in mid-January he cast off the docklines and headed out. A few days later he was already wishing for the old millennium.

In big seas and bigger winds, the shackle at the head of the mainsail had opened, and his halyard was soon enraptured with the top of the mast, and refused to let go. He managed to jury rig the topping lift to the mainsail but at a hazardous cost, because it had tangled with the errant main halyard and jammed the sail in the hoisted position. However, since it was in its second reef configuration, the boat wasn't overpowered. Peter fervently hoped the wind would not increase during the coming night. So, naturally, it did.

He stayed up all night and tended his Jeanneau 38 as she screamed along at speeds she had never before attained. At one point the GPS showed 10 knots. She was certainly displaying what a strong and speedy sailboat she was. But apparently she was not displaying herself very well as a radar target.

At 0700, when Peter stepped up into the cockpit to survey the horizon, it had been replaced by an onrushing wall of merciless steel. The tanker was so close that Peter could not even take evasive action. All he had time for was to vault down into the cabin and brace for the impact.

The behemoth slammed the sloop's bow with such force that it bent the pulpit all the way down to the waterline. This was quite a feat since it was still attached to the deck. It now looked like a cross between a mangled ladder and bank lobby sculpture. Then Peter's boat scraped down the hull of the tanker until the next wave swung them apart. Naturally the following wave swung them back together again - with extreme prejudice. The mast now joined the bow pulpit in the ocean. It, too, remained attached to the wounded sloop, in this case by a writhing web of stainless-steel wire. Since masts are creatures of the sky rather than the sea, they tend to react to that watery element by attacking the nearest fiberglass object that they can find.

But as dangerous as more holes in the hull might seem, there was an even more grisly threat rapidly approaching from astern. The little sloop was sliding down the tanker's waterline directly toward the very fangs of the beast, its churning propeller. As the two vessels rolled in the waves, Peter could actually see the huge, bronze prop rising out of the water, spewing a horizontal geyser of saltwater. He could only hope that it wouldn't soon be spitting bones, blood, and fiberglass as well.

With only yards to spare, he caught a break, which saved him from becoming the 'smoothie of the day.' The sea rolled him away from this petro-demon and into safe water. As he swept past the tanker, he got a clear and unforgettable view of the name painted on the stern: *Theodorus IV*. Armed with that information, but disarmed by the lack of an antenna, which was at the top of the mast and currently being baptized, Peter tried to radio the ship and ask for help.

When they did not respond, his tone became a bit more ada-mant, which, in this case, might be defined as pissed off to the 10th power. But neither the polite nor the perturbed approach worked. The tanker just steamed away. Staring at the departing vessel in rigid disbelief was the natural reaction, but he was quickly forced back into action by the stainless-steel rigging. Just because it was no longer standing did not mean that it was just lying around relaxing. In fact, it was whipping across the deck at ankle height with ferocious malice. Meanwhile the mast was thrashing away in the water, trying to convert his sloop into a colander.

This is perhaps a good time to mention the name that Peter had chosen for his boat. It was *Sozinho*, which is a Portuguese word, selected because of his ancestry. The loose translation means 'to live alone, or be by oneself.' And if ever he felt solitary, it was right now. Indeed, the most accurate translation at that moment was probably 'way out there and very alone.'

Aside from human fellowship, Peter was also craving the companionship of an oversized set of bolt cutters, which he did not possess. Instead, he began to dismantle the rigging by removing the cotter pins. This is often a frustrating task when performed on a stable boat, tied to a dock. In his current circumstances, with the boat flailing as wildly as a television evangelist with the phone bank idle, disconnecting the puny cotter pins was a gargantuan task.

And when he dropped some of his tools overboard, the job became the proverbial impossible dream. Losing the pliers was not due to negligence or klutzigence, but due to the fact that he was sliding across a deck that had been purged of lifelines, and he desperately needed to free up his hands to grab something. Next, he went at his rigging with a hacksaw, but because of the fiendish motion of the boat, it seemed like he was polishing the wires rather than severing them. His spirits were now as low as his overboard tools, but suddenly it dawned on him: these were Sta-Lok fittings. This meant that he could dismantle them by simply unscrewing them.

About two hours after the collision, he finished amputating his mast and rigging. He knelt on deck and watched as it silently sank. Its slow, irreversible spiral into the deep was perversely mesmerizing. But it was also traumatizing since it meant that his primary means of propulsion was gone. So now he needed to attend to his secondary means of propulsion.

Previously in this voyage he had experienced problems with his engine overheating, but he found that if he ran it for about 45 minutes and shut it down for 15 minutes, it would stay cool enough to ease him toward the nearest land, which was Bermuda, about 120 miles away. If the wind and wave conditions did not deteriorate any further, he figured that the shattered sloop and staggered skipper could make it to safety in 30 to 40 hours.

What he did not figure was that the tanker would return - but there she was heading back towards him. The optimist in Peter hoped that *Theodorus IV* was on a mission of mercy. The pessimist in him wondered if she was returning to 'finish the job.' His cynical voice cautioned that perhaps the captain had contacted the home office, and they had contacted their insurance company, and they had contacted their lawyers. If so, maybe they had decided that 'disposal' would be more cost-effective than litigation. But his trusting voice reassured him that they had probably returned to lend assistance.

Before his already tenuous mental stability could be frazzled even more, Peter heard a rich, Greek-accented voice hailing him on his handheld radio. After the initial shock of the collision, he remembered that he had one of those waterproof units stashed in his abandon-ship duffel bag. The ship's master was calling and apologizing with great fervor. The sincerity of his regret was made even more convincing when he offered to alter his course from Bangor to Bermuda, in order to escort *Sozinho* to safe refuge. Finally, it seemed like the Sky Bosun was smiling on Peter and his wounded yacht. But if so, it was a mischievous smile; because in a matter of hours his situation would Deteriorate with a capital D.

The tanker assumed an escort position about 100 yards off *Sozinho's* starboard side. During daylight this was a simple enough tactic, but at night it was much more difficult because the yacht with no mast and her decks nuked of hardware, was invisible on the radar screen in the big seas that were also escorting her. The captain and crew wisely compensated for this by keeping the ship's powerful spotlight focused on the little, lame sailboat.

But apparently, during a change of watch, when one spotlight operator was relieving another, the beam of light strayed from *Sozinho*. And before you could say, 'petro-lightning never strikes twice,' *the tanker slammed the luckless sloop again!*

This time the impact was in the stern and cockpit area. And this time the damage was terminal. She didn't sink in 90 seconds like most boats seem to do in liferaft survival stories. Instead, it took several hours for her leaks to overwhelm her pumps. Peter struggled valiantly during that time trying to repel the inevitable. But his two rounds of World Wrecking Federation Tankermania had punctured the boat in so many places that the electric bilge pump couldn't keep up. It was as impotent as Arizona during a Viagra shortage.

For a while Peter's labors at the manual bilge pump seemed to stabilize the situation, but Mother Ocean can be both relentless and remorseless. Even if The Village People had been there beside him, pumping away with manly vigor, the leaks were just too insurmountable. *Sozinho*, the love and joy of Peter's bachelor life, was going down.

Fortunately, he could not dwell on this for long, because he would soon have to be going up. Way up the tanker's vertical wall of steel, rivets, and rust while climbing a wildly swaying rope ladder. But before attempting such a treacherous boat-to-ship transfer, Peter asked the ship's master to radio Bermuda and see if the helicopter at the U.S. Navy base was available for his rescue. But the helo was no longer stationed there.

Peter realized that he would need both hands for the dangerous ascent, so he chose a bag with a shoulder strap for the few belongings that he would take with him. The satchel was barely big enough to hold a respectable watermelon. He grabbed his passport, ship's papers, money, the final few pages from his logbook and a few other valuables. Seven tons of life's mementos would soon sink to the ocean floor. Only seven pounds would survive.

Even though the ship's master did his best to minimize the rolling of the tanker as it made its final approach, the seas were too big and confused. But even if it had been a perfectly calm day, the transfer would have still been impossible for anyone who was not a world-class pole-vaulter. That's because the Jacob's ladder was about 15 feet too short. Seeing this, the crew started to position it further aft where the ship was lower, while the captain began maneuvering the ship around in a big circle to make another pass.

Realizing that he was in no way related to the Flying Wallendas, Peter was justifiably nervous about grabbing and climbing that ladder of thrills. But just in the nautical nick of time, the Bermuda Marine and Pilot Service offered to send out their fastest boat. That was the good news. The bad news was that it would take about six hours. Peter wondered whether he could keep pumping for that long. He also worried about the electric bilge pump, which could short out at any moment as the water rose in the cabin.

But gallant *Sozinho* remained loyal to the very end and refused to sink until the rescue boat arrived. To Peter in his dazed condition, the approaching craft seemed totally surreal as it came bounding over and crashing through the waves. It looked like it was from Andromeda rather than Bermuda. That's because it was one of those 'rollover' boats with the crew so dramatically helmeted and harnessed that they look like the heroes of a modern 'swashbuckler in bondage' movie. But they proved to be extremely skillful heavy-weather seamen as they quickly plucked Peter from his drowning boat, whose cabin was now at hot-tub depth.

The captain of *Theodorus IV*, seeing that the captain of *Sozinho* was now safe, returned to his original course and headed for

Maine. Before doing so, he gave Peter all of the important information that would allow him to contact the shipping company and make a damage claim. This was vital since, like most single-handed sea gypsies, Peter was essentially uninsurable and thus carried no coverage. Instead, he was forced to rely on the kindness of colliding vessels.

And speaking of kindness, he was treated superbly in Bermuda. His return to land in the rescue boat received full media coverage. This inspired an outpouring of heartwarming generosity from the local citizens. He was even provided free housing at the local Mariner's Club, which assists sailors when they are in distress.

So it appears that this tale has a happy ending since even though his beloved boat sank, the skipper did not. Indeed, he lived to tell what is possibly a unique sea story, in which a sailboat gets smashed by a tanker - twice - and all hands survive!

But there is an even happier ending to this astonishing saga. That's because I heard this story from Peter himself, whom I met one day as he was strolling down the dock where my lovely *Aventura* is berthed. And what was he doing at the Miami Beach Marina only a week after his return from Bermuda?

He was looking for a new boat to buy! Which unquestionably proves that Peter Augusto is either a fool or a hero. And I don't write stories about fools!

A Celery Fish

I've got a bad case of the Singlehanded TransPac blues. That's because last month those solo sailors set off across the Pacific bound for Kauai and they left without me. I did this race in 1990 and it was one of the highlights of my life. The fellowship with the skippers, the successful completion of the race, and the weeks of cleansing solitude all wove a web of enchantment around me.

And so I lament the fact that *Aventura* and I are not once again heading for the village by the bay at Hanalei. Well, what better way to chase away the blues than by sharing a story with some friends? And since I'm in a Hawaiian state of mind, I'll tell you about the first time that I sailed to those tall, trade-wind isles.

I was not single-handing on that voyage. My crewman was Terry Cassidy. He was also my best friend. We met in college when we were partners on the debate team, or as he liked to say, "when we were master debaters." He had a wonderfully skewed sense of humor that he brought to both the podium and the world.

I got my first glimpse of this during a practice match when he kept substantiating his arguments with very convincing quotes from a certain John E. Hoover. This befuddled our opponents who were frantically rifling through their file boxes searching for this source. Sure enough they fell into his trap; during their rebuttal they accused Terry of making up quotations to support his position. My turn came next, and I calmly informed them that John E. Hoover is also known as J. Edgar Hoover. Point and match went to Cassidy/Jason.

Since our friendship had not just survived, but actually flourished in the pressure-packed world of collegiate debating, I knew that we would do fine as a cruising team. And we certainly did. Our compatibility was excellent and entertaining.

We had decided to alternate cooking and dishwashing chores during our voyage. Under this system, one person prepared the meal and the other did the dishes. About halfway to Hawaii, I noticed that I was doing a lot of dishwashing and very little cooking. When I questioned my able crewman about this, his answer was "Self defense!"

He softened this direct but honest blow to my culinary skills by complimenting my tuna salad recipe. He said that he admired the purity of its composition: "One can of tuna, mixed with one jar of mayonnaise." Hey, they were really little jars!

Our passage to Hilo took a little over three weeks. We were both bemused and bruised by the experience. That's because it wasn't at all like the glossy magazines depict a trade-wind voyage to be. It wasn't just blue skies and cottonball clouds with a gentle breeze propelling us smoothly along. Instead it was mostly gray, snarling clouds with a relentlessly stiff wind and big, quartering seas. The pitching and yawing of the boat was so extreme that we thought we were on a thrill ride in a theme park in Purgatory. Burning in hell began to seem like a preferable option.

But we made it in one piece and a dozen bruises. Other sailors who did the trip from the West Coast to Hawaii that season didn't fare as well. They were OK physically but they were wounded psychologically. Many of them claimed that they would have sold their boats for 25 cents on the dollar.

Once we tied up to the seawall in Radio Bay and got checked in, we headed for town. My first impression of Hilo was that it was damp, dilapidated, and wonderful. I loved its bedraggled timeless-ness. Besides generally perusing the town, we were specifically in search of a sushi bar.

We had tried to catch our own fish in hopes of fresh sashimi during our passage across the Pacific. But we had zero success. We would see them swimming beside our lures, apparently admiring the craftsmanship of these plastic and chrome imposters. But the fish were too intelligent to bite. After a while, Terry would begin each morning by proclaiming, "Today is the day that I am going to catch the great white Mensa Fish!"

Not only did we find some excellent sushi on that first day's exploration of Hilo, but we also made a new friend. Her name was Peggy, and as nautical coincidence would have it, she was working at a motel that was owned by a couple who had circumnavigated their backyard-built sailboat. This was perfect, since we could now ask some veteran cruisers whether the extremely rolly, uncomfort-able conditions that we experienced on our first ocean crossing were normal.

We gathered at their place, which, if I recall correctly, was called the Blue Dolphin Motel. It could just as easily have been called the Extremely Self-Reliant Motel. That's because this wonderful couple had not only built their boat by themselves, they had also built their *motel* by themselves.

They regaled us with great tales from the days when the number of cruisers was in the dozens rather than in the thousands. They spoke of pioneer voyaging couples like the Hiscocks and the Smeetons, and of a young single-hander named Robin Lee Graham. It was an inspiring and magical night.

Eventually, when things were starting to wind down, Terry popped the question that we so desperately wanted to ask. "During your circumnavigation, what percentage of the passage-making days were idyllic and what portion were uncomfortable or downright terrifying?"

In their slow, thoughtful manner, they both paused for about 30 seconds. Then, almost in unison they said, "Oh, yeah, there was that *one* lovely day in the Indian Ocean." Terry groaned and said, "Sounds like we better double the daily rum ration!"

A few days later we sailed off on a pilgrimage. We were going to visit the monument that marks the spot where Captain Cook was killed. Terry and I were in awe of this man. We felt that he deserved to be ranked amongst the greatest human beings of all time. He was a bold explorer who dealt with icebergs, reefs, and cannibals. He was an extraordinary navigator whose chart making was incredibly accurate, especially considering the primitive instruments that he had to work with. And he was a superb leader who combined his expertise in such varied disciplines as botany, diplomacy, medicine, and languages.

As we approached Kealakekua Bay, Terry and I decided to anchor farther out than we normally would. Even though this would require a longer row to the monument, we wanted to position *Aventura* as close as possible to where Captain Cook had probably anchored his ships.

We rowed silently over to the obelisk that marks the fatal spot, and paid our heartfelt respects to this superlative seaman and human. Then we stroked the old, gray dinghy across the bay to the little beach and sat quietly under the trees. Eventually, I ended our reverie by commenting on how fitting it was that the names of the last two vessels that Captain Cook commanded so perfectly represented two of the defining qualities of his own life. The names of those ships were *Resolution* and *Discovery.*

Then Terry touched my heart by saying, "You may not know it, Ray, but I'm really proud to be crewing on a boat whose name so perfectly captures your spirit and quest - *Aventura*, Spanish for adventure." I looked over at my friend of over 20 years and thanked him with my eyes. I was expressing gratitude not just for that wonderful compliment, but also for the decades of fellowship that we had shared. Even though we had been in hundreds of debates, never once had there been a serious or hurtful argument between the two of us.

Inspired by the spirit of Captain Cook, Terry and I sat on the beach for another hour, quietly discussing the glory and folly of human endeavor. But our philosophical dialogue was rudely shattered by an outbreak of PWC - personal watercraft. A vile jet ski came blasting into the bay, destroying our perfect tranquility with a grotesque shriek that sounded like a man taking a chainsaw to a tin roof.

After observing this screeching, snorting beast for a few minutes, I said to my friend, "If you ever see me on one of those things, shoot me!" And then, almost as if on cue, a man walked onto the beach with a metal detector and started scanning the sand in search of precious bottle caps and costume jewelry. Seeing this,

Terry said, "And Ray, if you ever see me doing that, torture me before you shoot me!"

Since our paradise was now thoroughly jangled and definitely lost, it was time to leave. We headed our bow up the Kona Coast in search of a hidden marina that I had heard about. Usually, I prefer to be on the hook, but in a few days my sweetheart, Hillary, was flying in for a visit. Since I planned to rent a car so that we could do extensive onshore exploring, I would feel better if *Aventura* was secured in a marina.

The problem was that the only facility that was available catered almost exclusively to sportsfishing boats. However, exceptions were made for sailing vessels with mechanical failures. So we created a marine diesel melodrama. We entered the little harbor, which had literally been blasted out of an old lava flow, and instead of motoring into a slip, we sailed into the middle of the basin and anchored. This demonstrated to the harbormaster the severity of our situation. Then I rowed ashore and visited the office in search of mercy. I was granted a marina slip for a week, in order to effect repairs.

The morning that Hillary arrived, I could be seen suspiciously arranging rocks beside the road that led from the highway to the marina. I was imitating a local high-school custom whereby the kids express their affection for each other by spelling out messages using lava chunks. But instead of saying 'Danny loves Julie' or 'Tommy and Angela' my sign proclaimed 'Ray Loves Celery.'

This enigmatic message must have been a real mind bender for the fishermen who frequented this road. Did they interpret it as some rallying cry to vegetarianism? What it actually referred to was Hillary's childhood nickname, which was Celery.

I had met this wonderful young woman at a *Latitude 38* crew-list party; so how could I not fall in love with her? We were compatible in so many ways with one significant exception. I was free to sail across the horizon and she was not. If she had been constrained by any normal job, I would have probably tried to talk her into leaving it. But she was doing valuable, enjoyable work that made a positive difference in people's lives. She was the Special Events Coordinator at the Exploratorium. So she devoted her workdays to introducing thousands of people to this terrific, hands-on science museum.

After Hillary arrived, we spent the next several days wandering around the amazing island of Hawaii in a rental car. We quickly learned why the locals insist that the Big Island is 'mo bettah!' We were dazzled by its extraordinary diversity. We visited ancient, dried-up lava fields and brand-new, active volcanic vents. We sampled macadamia nuts and coffee beans right at the plantations where they were grown. We saw cattle ranches, sugar-cane fields, and orchid fields only short drives away from each other.

We marveled at an island that is soggy on one side and dry on the other. We were enchanted by mighty Mauna Kea, which is tropical at its base and ski-able at its summit. We listened and danced to their gorgeous music. And to top it all off, the friendliness of the locals was as genuine and constant as the trade wind that cools the fragrant evenings.

The allurements of the Big Island were so overwhelming that it was difficult to stick to our budget. So we started looking for ways to reef down our expenses. Hillary found a great one. The mate on an enormous sportsfishing boat in the slip next to us suggested that we visit the fish house at the end of the day, because some of the fishermen toss away their bait. Since these guys are routinely going after marlin that weigh hundreds of pounds, they use fairly sizable baitfish.

On our very first attempt we scored a five-pound tuna. They

even gave us a clear, plastic bag in which to tote it back to
Aventura. Once aboard, I put some briquettes in the stern barbecue,
while Celery went down into the galley and began preparing the
rest of our dinner.

A little while later, the mate from the boat next to us arrived
with two prospective buyers. The gigantic, state-of-the-art
sportsfisher had just gone on the market, and people were even
flying in from the mainland to look her over. The two guys with
him looked about as nautical as Siskel and Ebert, but they certainly
looked rich. However, I should mention that I also looked pretty
snazzy at that moment.

That's because I was wearing what I call my Supplication
Clothes. This is the one good outfit that I own. Normally, I don it
only when I'm visiting customs officers, seeking a visa extension,
or trying to sneak into a toney resort. In this case I had worn it
when Hillary and I went begging for a not-too-old fish. The en-
semble consists of khaki long pants, the deck shoes that I don't
wear during oil changes, a belt with a scrimshaw buckle and a polo
shirt without a designer logo.

After showing the potential buyers around our neighboring
yacht, the mate hollered over to me and asked whether we had
gone searching for free fish, as he had suggested. Upon hearing
this, Hillary came rushing up from the cabin with our little trophy.
She stood up beside me on the cockpit seat with the tuna hidden
behind her back.

Perhaps it was the sight of the Corporate Warriors in their
expensive suits, sweltering in the tropical sun that broke her concentration. Or perhaps it was just her wonderful enthusiasm towards life in general. But whatever it was, when she used her best
magician's flourish to reveal our humble fish, she did so with the
bag turned upside down. So the fish dropped into the water be-

tween our two boats.

Without a second's hesitation I dove over the lifelines into the water in pursuit of our prize. I actually beat it to the bottom, so it was an easy catch. When I burst to the surface with the fish held proudly in my upraised hand; Hillary applauded like a teenager who had just been given her own phone.

The two men in the suits were astonished. They couldn't seem to speak or move. Sensing that I needed to do something to break the spell, I looked over at them and offered an explanation. "I had to do it guys. I didn't really have a choice. You see… it is an extremely rare Celery Fish!"

The Pancake Test

When searching for the Truth, I often whip up a batch of banana pancakes. If someone spins a particularly good yarn at a waterfront bar, I invite them to my sailboat for breakfast the next day. While stirring the pancake batter, I slyly encourage them to retell the tale from the previous night. If the breakfast version is similar to the happy-hour rendition, chances are that there is some truth in there somewhere.

This particular pancake test was being conducted at a very exotic locale, the threshold of the Panama Canal. My 30-foot sloop *Aventura* was attached to a far-out mooring buoy at the Balboa Yacht Club, on the Pacific Ocean side of the canal. Admittedly, describing a mooring buoy as far-out might seem a bit extreme, even for a San Franciscan like myself; but in this case it was not an exaggeration. In fact, it was far-out in three ways.

First, because it was in the row of moorings farthest from the clubhouse. Since all visiting sailors are required to use the shuttle service rather than their own dinghies when traveling from yacht to yacht club, being far outside was a significant disadvantage. Particularly since getting the attention of the shuttle drivers was only slightly less difficult than achieving lasting peace in the Middle East.

The standard method employed by most skippers was to alternate between waving their arms frantically and blowing their air horns. While waving, the logical place to put the frigid air-horn canister was between their legs; which inspired some exceedingly vigorous arm movements. At night, the situation was even more difficult. You might be heard, but you couldn't be seen. To offset this, many sailors tried getting the shuttle jockey's attention by turning on their masthead strobe lights. This made it look like the anchorage had contracted disco fever.

Eventually, I hit upon the perfect solution: *Flor de Cana.* This is Spanish for 'Flower of the Cane,' which is Nicaraguan for fine, cheap, dark rum. I had purchased a case at a duty-free outlet in Costa Rica for just such nautical contingencies. A single bottle, slipped to the chief shuttle driver, did the trick.

Once it actually arrived at your boat, the shuttle made quite an impression. The craft itself was about 25-feet long. In the middle was The Beast, a one-cylinder diesel engine whose revolutions were as slow as the pulse of a Galapagos tortoise. But what it lacked in crankshaft speed, it made up for in noise. It was so loud that you would swear it was a tramp steamer whose turbo-diesel had gone five oceans between oil changes. There was nothing subtle about this shuttle.

The second reason that my mooring was far out was actually quite enchanting. For although *Aventura* was farthest away from the clubhouse, she was nearest to the channel. So less than 100 feet away, day and night, I was treated to a throbbing steel cavalcade, as some of the world's mightiest ships promenaded past my humble sloop. For a full-rigged romantic like myself, with blue water in my veins and Conrad in my back pocket, this was a procession of exquisite majesty.

The third reason was related to the second one. As this mighty armada of cargo and crude passed by, they altered the fluid dynamics of the surrounding area. In other words, those big suckers set up some humongous wakes. One instant *Aventura's* stern would be far out of the water and the next moment her bow would be far out. It was more turbulent than a hot tub full of open-marriage advocates.

But enough descriptive detours; back to the 'pancake test.' Seated at *Aventura's* saloon table were Earl, the skipper and owner of *Running Free*, and his crewmember Vincent, named after a fellow Dutchman who was a painter of some renown. They were regaling me again with the tale of their Voyage of Agony from Costa Rica to the Panama Canal. I had done this trip single-handed at around the same time. It had taken me about six days. It took them six days plus two weeks. For them it was nearly the trip of a lifetime - the final trip of a lifetime.

It began favorably enough for their Columbia 38 with a moderate breeze from astern. Although the wind was strong enough to move them along at five knots, Earl also ran the engine in order to charge up the batteries. Since the course from the Gulf of Nicoya to the canal runs right down the shipping lanes, he would need his running lights at night.

Only four hours after their departure, the engine stopped. It gave no warning whatsoever. It just ceased to operate. Earl, who already had far too much practice at repairing this engine, was now faced with an interesting decision. They had gone 20 nautical miles and there were 430 left to go. The wind was favorable and he could probably fix the engine in a few hours. So, sounding very much like the bogus bravado of television advertising, he announced that they would 'go for it!' Weeks later, it would seem to him more like he had 'gone through it' or 'stepped in it.'

Vincent, who had never sailed before and who was backpacking around the world when he signed on as crew, was dazzled by Earl's display of boldness. It was just like in the movies, he thought to himself. That night it turned into a horror movie.

Earl worked all afternoon on the engine. He tried the affectionate, coddling approach: 'Nice, trusty Perkins marine diesel.' And he also used the frustrated, desperate method : 'Vile, scum of the sea Perkins.' But neither tactic worked. The engine wouldn't run. At nightfall he decided to discontinue his efforts until first light the next day. This was a wise choice since things were getting a bit crowded and nerve-racking in the neighborhood. As night descended, so did the wind velocity. This meant that their ability to steer *Running Free* was dropping faster than a Sumo skydiver.

Thus far, the wounded sloop had behaved admirably by choosing to meander inside the shipping lanes and outside the shrimp boats. But the first squall of the night shoved them out toward the big boys, the big, *bad* boys. Now, valuable battery power had to be expended on the navigation light at the top of the mast. But even that wasn't enough when 700 feet of disaster approached them at 0300. Earl was on watch. He could see a ship nearing them, but it looked like it would pass by them safely. His fear was that the next squall, which was approaching, might push them towards a collision.

He blinked his mast light off and on several times, hoping that it would alert the officers on the bridge. He then made a mental note to add a masthead strobe light and a high-powered spotlight to his Christmas wish list. With either of those he would have a much better chance of signaling a ship.

Then the squall hit. The rain came down so forcefully that it was physically painful. Earl's vision was completely obscured, and it frightened him deeply. In fact, his fear was so primal that he could feel a chill at the base of his spine. Its icy energy reconnected him across the millennia with his primitive ancestors trembling in their caves while a tiger roared at the entrance.

He hurried below and woke up Vincent. He tried to contact the ship on the radio, but no luck. He tried again, still no luck. Then he noticed that the radio was humming, or throbbing, or vibrating, or something. He finally realized that the throbbing was the ship's engine. And it was getting much louder much too quickly.

Earl grabbed the flare-gun canister and raced topside. Vincent was right behind him. They both shouted the 'S' word at the same time. Not because they could actually see the ship through the hellacious downpour, but because they could feel it coming toward them out of the darkness. Earl managed to get a flare into the gun and shoot it skyward. But suddenly the sky was rudely replaced by the bow of the ship.

The red skyrocket spewed 30 feet into the air, and then with a sizzling clunk, it ricocheted off the bow of the beast just below her anchor. During that terrifying instant they could clearly see the name of the ship. It was *Joyous Mankind.*

Then the bow wave pushed *Running Free* nearly horizontal. When she straightened up she pivoted 180 degrees and started wallowing backward down the side of the monster. If she rotated again she would surely be puréed in its propeller. But she spun no more; and slid by unharmed.

The crew of the barely spared sloop shivered in the rain. Not that it was cold so close to the equator. Paradoxically, they trembled from the frigid chill of emotional meltdown. Vincent wondered if this was what sailing was like on a daily basis. Eventually, he verbalized his concern.

"Skipper, would that be considered a close call?"

"As close as it gets," responded Earl. "Any closer and we would have been propeller pulp."

"Whew, what a first night."

"Yeah, and it was almost our last night; our last night as members of joyous mankind."

"That was a pretty weird name for a ship," said Vincent.

"Well, at least we know it was Chinese," responded Earl.

"Why's that?"

"Because only the Chinese are inscrutable enough to name their ships after exalted, unattainable philosophical concepts."

Just after dawn, the wind returned and bequeathed them several hours of pleasant sailing. Earl returned to his engine investigation and made a sobering discovery: a valve had completely broken. There could be no jury rig. Even a jury filled with Mr. Goodwrenches couldn't repair this damage at sea.

There was only one port between *Running Free* and the Panama Canal where the engine might be fixed. So the skipper set a new course for Golfito, Costa Rica, which was 120 miles down the costa and 20 miles up the Golfo Dulce. Rollerblading up Mt. Everest would probably have been a more attainable goal. That's because the Wind God, the Current God, and the Fishing Boats That Might Give Them a Tow God were apparently finding Earl and Vincent's struggle quite entertaining. So the ill-fated sloop drifted past the Golfo Dulce and into Panamanian waters.

Trying to put a positive spin on a negative situation, Earl

emphasized that sailing off the coast of Panama was a vital step in getting to the Panama Canal. Spinning their predicament the other direction, Vincent pointed out that they had only made 150 nerve-racking miles in five days and they had 300 more miles to go. And since the batteries were almost dead, how would that affect things? What about their food and water supply?

Earl had to admit that Vincent's concerns were pretty sensible and levelheaded. So the two of them tried to evaluate how desperate their situation really was. Their biggest concern was how dependent they were on the boat's batteries. Once they were discharged, there would be no running lights for warning passing ships and no cabin lights for reading charts at night. Likewise there would be no radio or GPS or autopilot. But what was even more disturbing was that once the batteries couldn't open the propane solenoid, they wouldn't be able to cook. And worst of all, without the pressure pump, they wouldn't be able to get drinking water out of the sloop's tank.

Still trying to find a plus in a sea of minuses, Earl reminded Vincent that if the wind would just fill in, they could be at the canal in less than three days. Six days later, they were still ghosting along. Ghosting was probably very accurate in this case, seeing as how both skipper and crew were beginning to take on a pale, ghoulish appearance. Vincent even joked that Earl looked like the Phantom of the Ocean. The combination of shipping-lane stress, uncooked food, and minimal drinking water was taking a serious toll.

When they finally neared Cabo Malo they encountered windo malo. This cabo is one of those Cape Hatteras/Point Conception-type headlands that can be total agony to get around. It is the final corner one must turn to head up the Gulf of Panama to the canal entrance. The wind is almost always strong and 'noserly,' as is the current, which can exceed 2 knots.

Earl and Vincent and *Running Free* valiantly slammed to windward for nearly three days before admitting defeat. Reluctantly, they altered course for the Las Perlas Islands, a more attainable goal since they weren't nearly as far upwind. But even though they seemed to make progress, without the GPS they couldn't determine how severely the wind and current were deflecting them off course.

Apparently quite a bit, because the next land they spotted was Colombia. They gathered this information from a very well-dressed native who roared up to them in an interesting-looking 'fishing boat' that sported more antennas than Mission Control at NASA. In excellent English, he inquired what brought them to his neighborhood. When convinced of the innocence of their intrusion, he gave them their position and some other helpful navigational information.

Politely, they asked if he could spare some water. He had none, but instead he handed them a six-pack of ice-cold Heineken beer. Vincent, being from Holland, was so overwhelmed by this gesture, that he began thanking the man profusely in his native tongue. This might have flustered some people, but this Colombian 'fisherman' seemed accustomed to the spectacle of someone prostrating himself and blabbering uncontrollably in his presence. When Vincent was done, the man roared away.

And so *Running Free* again set a course for the Panama Canal, if bobbing around becalmed can be so described. But at least on this side of the Gulf of Panama the current was with them rather than against them. This was a very good thing because their food and water situation had become truly desperate.

After the beer was gone and the emergency water had been

exhausted, they survived by opening canned vegetables and drinking the fluid. Vincent hit on the idea of making this noxious liquid more palatable by mixing it with Tang. Earl began to wonder if dehydration was pushing them over the brink when Vincent suggested a blind taste test to see if they could discern green-bean water from French-style green-bean water. They were down to eating Top Ramen - dry Top Ramen! They tried soaking it in vegetable juice, but found that combination even more loathsome. So they used it like rice cakes. Vincent swore that when compared to real rice cakes, the dry Top Ramen was as moist as watermelon.

Eventually, this oceanic soap opera came to an end. Naturally, the final act was as tragi-comic as the rest of their voyage. They were tacking up the narrow channel leading to the moorings at the Balboa Yacht Club. The wind was snotty, and as is appropriate with such an adjective, it was on the nose. Each tack across the channel seemed to coincide with the arrival of a huge ship. But straying outside this narrow area meant going aground. Twice, in order to avoid imminent collision, they had to quickly reverse their course, losing hard-won upwind progress each time.

At long last, they were able to pass close enough to another sailboat to ask them to radio the yacht club for help. Ten minutes later, one of the shuttle boats with the tramp-steamer engines was heaving them a line and taking them in tow. Two minutes after that, the shuttle ran out of fuel and the two boats, now locked in towus-interruptus, were drifting down current. Naturally, they were aimed directly between the two gleaming hulls of a luxury catamaran on a nearby mooring.

Less than a minute before impact, they were rescued by a small Panamanian fishing boat. The fisherfolk in this craft were smart enough to not attempt a tow. Instead, they just pushed the two-boat tangle clear of the catamaran and let it drift down current until it went aground. The yacht club dispatched another shuttle with spare diesel fuel to the scene. Then they pulled *Running Free* off the mud, tied her up to a mooring buoy and ferried the bedraggled sailors to the club where they feasted on warm food and cold beer - compliments of the house.

After finishing the retelling of their harrowing tale, Earl looked across at me and said, "Ray, you just can't imagine how moist and delicious these pancakes taste after a diet of dry Top Ramen."

To which Vincent added, "And without a doubt, this fresh-squeezed orange juice tastes like the nectar of the gods compared to beet juice and Tang."

Delighted and inspired by these living, laughing examples of the sturdiness of the human spirit, I reached into a nearby cabinet and removed a bottle. Then to toast the tenacity of these stalwart sailors, I poured us all a healthy dollop of the Flower of the Cane.

Disco Sea Fever

My boat features moveable ballast in its most primitive form. Stowed in the bilge are three full-sized bowling balls. But their purpose is not to provide extra stability in rough seas for my 30-foot sloop, *Aventura*. Instead, they are used to mesmerize the natives in foreign locales. That's because not only am I a sea gypsy, I'm also a vagabond juggler who periodically tops off the cruising kitty by performing my show in strange and exotic settings. Some of these experiences are certifiably memorable. Perhaps I could share one of them with you.

Not only were we frustrated, we were saturated. All morning long we had attempted to pioneer a new system that we had dubbed 'crowbar anchoring.' Because the bottom of the bay was composed of just a few feet of hard-packed sand over many feet of centuries-packed coral, it was extremely difficult to get an anchor to set. So Peter and I were experimenting with an unusual technique for getting the hook to dig in. One of us would snorkel down 15 feet and scrape a short trench behind my 35-pound CQR with a crowbar. Then the person at the tiller would back the boat down while the in-the-water accomplice watched through his swim mask to see if the anchor set.

Repeatedly we tried this technique with each of us taking turns in the water. After two hours and zero success, our patience was as wrinkled as our skin. No matter how nice a furrow we scraped into the sand, my plow anchor just wouldn't live up to its name and dig in.

So why not just give up and anchor elsewhere? Because this particular cove belonged to a beautiful Club Med that had just hired me to juggle for their guests. And for a single-handed bachelor who had been so solo for so long, this was like a Sailor's Valhalla - or even better, a Galhalla! So I was determined to get *Aventura* securely situated. I was equally determined to get her skipper supremely satiated. And to insure Peter's help in my anchor quest, I had promised that he and his family could spend a day at Club Med as my guests.

Peter and his crew were some of my favorite sailors in the entire Mexican cruising fleet. Because there were six people aboard his boat and one aboard mine, we were definitely at the opposite ends of the voyaging spectrum. According to my informal calculations, it seemed that about 85 percent of the cruising fraternity were couples, while 10 percent were families and 5 percent were singlehanders. Of the family group, only the boat *Blaze* had four kids aboard. What made things even more challenging was that the kids were between the ages of four and ten.

When I playfully quizzed Molly about what sort of birth control she and Peter used, she laughed and said that because of their Catholic upbringing, they employed the rhythm method. Sensitive human being that I am, it seemed only appropriate to immediately nickname her husband 'The Rhythm Master.'

Their kids were a total delight. They were bright, healthy, inquisitive, playful, and nice to each other. They could have been poster children for any crusade to prove that home-schooled youngsters enjoying the sea gypsy life were better off than kids raised in the so-called 'real world.' Needless to say, as both a juggler and a storyteller it wasn't difficult to win their friendship, and many memorable and magical times were shared aboard the bright red sloop named *Blaze*.

Eventually, Peter and I solved my anchoring problem, not with the crowbar but with a 300-pound slab of concrete. It was an abandoned block that the club's scuba boats had once used as a mooring. I guessed that the management wouldn't object to my recycling this into a new mooring, and indeed they didn't. This meant that I could safely move ashore for a few weeks, and still watch over my fiberglass sweetheart from my window. Perfection!

During my stay at the club, they had what they referred to as a 'special week.' For six days the facility was exclusively booked by a gay travel company. This meant that there were approximately 600 homosexual men and the 50 or so heterosexual staff members. As a person who had spent more than 20 years in San Francisco, this was certainly not bothersome to me. Indeed, watching their mating rituals from the sidelines was quite entertaining. For example, they all wore chrome-plated designer 'dog tags' around their necks with colored stick-on dots to indicate their availability status. A red spot stood for 'Partnered off, don't waste your time.' Yellow translated to 'Not sure, buy me a drink and we'll see what happens.' Green implied 'Good to go.' And two green spots meant

'Meet me in my room in 10 minutes. You can tell me your name then.'

Apparently the Sky Bosun thought that Gay Week would provide a wonderful opportunity to play a little joke on two cruisers anchored nearby. This couple had flown down to stay at the club a few years earlier. During that vacation, they met some cruising sailors whose healthy, adventurous, and happy voyaging proved so alluring that the couple decided to go cruising themselves. So they bought a good boat, cut themselves free of society's web and headed out.

Naturally, one of the stops that they most looked forward to was the Club Med where this life-changing idea had been born. Since anchoring is not allowed directly in front of the club, they dropped their hook in the cove just around the headland, where the ocean boats congregate. They cooked a meal and then rested in preparation for that night's triumphant return, which they planned to celebrate at the disco. And indeed there was genuine cause for their jubilation, because many people fantasize about going cruising, but few actually cut the rope and set themselves free.

When they beached their dinghy that night, they were surprised by two things. First, there were no security guards in evidence. And second, there were no couples walking arm-in-arm along the beach in the moonlight. Their third surprise explained the first two mysteries. When they opened the door to the disco, they were greeted by a scene that looked like it could have been co-directed by the ghosts of Fellini and Liberace. Six hundred men were dancing in ecstatic abandon, clad only in their underwear. And their briefs were so brief that you could have probably fit all 600 pairs into one dinghy. To make it even more surreal, all the underwear was virginal white.

The husband, in a gesture of matrimonial gallantry closed the door, put his back against it and said, "What in the hell is going on in there?"

The wife, suppressing a giggle, said, "I don't know, but why don't we go in and find out? Don't worry, I'll protect you!"

So in they went. And what they learned was that this was Gay Week and tonight was White Party Night. But they also learned a more important lesson that almost all cruisers master: You have to sail with the wind you've got. Or as a landsman might say, "You have to adapt to the circumstances."

So they had a completely different 'homecoming' experience from the one that they had anticipated. But it was perhaps even more amazing, and certainly more memorable. As to whether or not the husband peeled down to his underwear and danced in ecstatic abandon with his delighted wife… well, perhaps you should ask them.

The Pacific Prankster

It was not a good day to die. Nor was it a good night to die. But it certainly felt like I was locked in hand-to-hand combat with Admiral Reaper. Actually, hand-to-neck combat was the more accurate description.

When cruising sailors occasionally ponder the possibility of dying during a voyage, the scenarios that they usually conjure up tend to be boldly heroic. They imagine themselves battling Hurricane Attila to a stalemate or saving a virginal maiden from depraved Sulu Sea pirates. But being strangled by one's own dinghy is not the script that any sailor would willingly choose for his final farewell.

It all began with a visit to the Pacific Prankster. Philomena is her name and Pagliacci is her game. She is the clown princess of the Mexican cruising fleet. With a sense of whimsy like

Shakespeare's Puck, she holds court over one of the world's great cruiser havens. Every winter and spring, scores of sailboats anchor in front of her Melaque beachfront restaurant, Los Pelicanos, which is Spanish for - you guessed it - The Pelicans. There, Phil dishes out delicious meals at delectable prices. In the morning she runs the cruisers' radio net, which helps sailors locate diesel fuel, refrigeration repairmen, propane, refrigeration repairmen, groceries, refrigeration repairmen, and so on.

She is also guardian of The Wall. Or should that be Walls? Or better yet, Surfaces? That's because almost every square inch of her restaurant's interior is covered with painted logos from the many yachts that have visited. Leaving a memento at Los Pelicanos is an eagerly awaited rite of passage for most Mexican cruisers.

Many of the boat portraits are exquisitely rendered by crews who spend days painting a design that they hope will endure for posterity. Little do they realize that in Mexico, posterity fluctuates as dramatically as the peso. For if they visit the following season, it's likely that their masterpieces will have vanished under a new coat of white enamel. Philomena usually blames this on a leaky roof. Interestingly, the logos of boats that she knows will be returning the following season invariably seem to escape those pesky 'roof leaks.' Chances are that their designs will still be there when they come back. All the new boats, of course, have all of that freshly whitened wall space for their logos.

One last interesting little tidbit about The Wall, is the persistent rumor of spaghetti justice. Supposedly, Phil uses the logos of boats that have dropped from her favor to determine if her spaghetti is properly cooked. She simply flings a strand of pasta against their painting, a clever method of gaining retribution.

With a name like Philomena, you would figure that she is as

Mexican as Pancho Villa. But although her husband Trini is Mexican, Phil actually grew up north of the border. Her Spanish is machine-gun authentic and her English is not bad for someone raised in Philadelphia. Her restaurant is located at the Melaque end of Bahia de Navidad. Melaque, when pronounced correctly, rhymes with 'rocky,' which is most fitting, since it is one of the rolliest anchorages on the planet when the swell is coming from a southerly direction.

Most cruisers use a bow-and-stern, two-anchor strategy, facing into the waves. This approach has dual advantages. First, it lessens the uncomfortable motion, and second, it provides a better view of the dinghy rodeo. Because when the swell is running high, it sets up a ferocious shore break in front of Los Pelicanos. Anyone trying to land an inflatable through that surf should prepare to be launched higher than a rookie bronco rider at his first Grand National.

They should also be ready to perform these acrobatics in front of a large audience. That's because Phil has placed an old, cast-iron skillet and a wooden mallet by the side of the restaurant that faces the beach. Whenever an inflatable is approaching in conditions that might produce a somersault or at least a cartwheel, she starts clanging on the frying pan. This alerts the boats at anchor so that everyone can witness the surf-n'-turf spectacle.

A particularly good performance with lots of flailing and flying usually generates considerable horn applause from the fleet. Woodenboat purists, who are unwilling to defile their 'traditionals' with an air horn, would blow their conch shells to signal their approval of an especially choice lift-off.

The soggy and stunned recipients of this good-natured teasing are usually pretty easy-going about this abuse because they realize that eventually their tormentors will also get their chance to play dinghy crash dummy. Probably the reason that everyone makes an entertainment out of this is because of the genuine seriousness of the situation. A 50-pound outboard motor transformed into a projectile is extremely dangerous. And the propeller blades on those beasts can be sharp and nasty, like a zoot-suiter gone bad.

Furthermore, many cruising sailors don't know how to swim. If a backyard pool induces paralyzing fear for some of them, imagine the terror they experience while churning around, upside down in this Mexican Maytag. So, beneath the kidding there is sincere compassion. If anyone damages more than their pride, they receive lots of care and comfort. On some days at Melaque, the beach landings are so treacherous that nobody goes ashore. But that's why the Sky Bosun invented Happy-Hour Dinghy Raft-Ups.

The day of my inflatable disaster actually began quite pleasantly. There was no humongous swell rolling up from the equatorial regions, so rowing ashore had been painless. I spent the day hanging out with two friends in Barra de Navidad, which is the town across the bay from Melaque. Every winter this town shelters a very eccentric and eclectic group of American expatriates. I loved the place because it always gave me the impression that the Federal Witness Relocation Program was alive and well.

One of the friends that I was visiting was named Candido, which rhymes with 'bandito.' Observing his prowess with the señoritas, one realized that Candido also rhymes with 'randito.' After finishing the harvest every year for a Humboldt County agricultural combine, he would fly down and kick back.

His best friend's name had a bit less 'south of the border' zing to it. His name was Bob. Even without a mañana name, Bob had taken 'laid back' to another level. In fact, when I first saw him, he was so motionless that I thought he was a scarecrow. An upscale scarecrow though, because atop that tall, lanky, immobile body was an expensive panama hat.

Bob was the lead singer and guitarist for a terrific group that played music most nights at a local hangout. He wore his hat so low that it covered all of his face except his mouth. That he kept hidden behind the microphone. But even though you couldn't see him very well, you could hear him just fine. And, my oh my, could that white boy ever play that reggae music! He was so good that you began to wonder if his full name might be Bob Ganja.

He had a superbly skewed way of looking at the world that I could easily relate to. Back in his high-school days, he and another friend, also named Bob, were holding auditions for a band they were putting together. After checking out a dozen musicians, they chose one named Lou and one named - Bob. They admitted that these two guys weren't the most talented of the try-outs, but because of their names, they could call their new group 'Bob, Bob, a Lou, Bob.'

During my time at Melaque I spent many a lively night at the club where Bob performed. It was called the Casa Blanca by the management, but Candido called it 'Casa Drunka.' It was there that he taught me the fine points of the Passive Prowl. Instead of rambling from bar to bar in search of adventure and romance, the three of us - four if you counted Jose Cuervo - would let the parade come to us. However, that evening I was heading back to Casa *Aventura* because the following day I had a snorkeling date with lovely Leah, the very same Leah that I had met during my run-in with the Macaroon Police.

Arriving back in Melaque by bus, I found Los Pelicanos filled with cruisers. They were in a loud and boisterous mood, but not so noisy that I didn't immediately notice the distinctive roar that meant 'surf's up!' The waves slamming onto the beach were nasty. They boomed like the tape-deck bass in a big-city lowrider. The swell had come up suddenly and strongly during the late afternoon. This meant that lots of cruisers had been stranded ashore. Everyone was waiting for the waves to go down a little. But since Phil had recently repaired her margarita blender, this was an easy choice.

Just after 10 p.m., a couple decided to brave the shore break and try to launch their dinghy. With a strong outboard, a rigid-bottomed inflatable, patience and teamwork, they timed it perfectly and made it safely out through the breakers. Encouraged by their success - or was Señor Cuervo my inspiration? - I also decided to give it a try.

Now my dinghy, *Ling*, does not have an outboard or a rigid bottom or even floorboards. Not having a motor makes it a lot less dangerous if it goes airborne, but a lot more difficult to launch. That's because you have to jump into the dink during a lull between waves and row like hell. If you make it to deep enough water before the next wave breaks, you've won the battle.

Not only did I lose the battle that night, but from my submerged and confused vantage point, it seemed like I was also losing the war. That's because instead of popping back up to the surface like I normally do if my dinghy cartwheels, I was somehow pinned underneath it. My new world was mostly pitch black except when a wave smashed it full of yellow/green phosphorescence. So in the darkness I couldn't see a way out of my trap. Hell, I couldn't even tell what I was tangled up in.

But just when the predicament of this air-breathing mammal trapped in a watery habitat was getting deadly serious, my head popped to the surface. Not only did the Sky Bosun bequeath me a feast of lung-soothing air, but I also got a quick glimpse of my entanglement.

There are ropes that run down the outsides of most inflatable dinghies. These grablines enable a sailor to drag or carry the boat. They are usually tightly sewn or glued to the side of the pontoons so that only your hands can fit though. But on *Ling* the middle attachment had broken off a few weeks earlier. In admirable Mexican fashion, I had put off repairing it until mañana. But as any veteran Mexican cruiser knows, mañana doesn't actually mean 'tomorrow.' It means 'Not now and probably not even soon.'

So my cavalier - or should that be caballero? - attitude had come back to haunt me. This wouldn't have been so bad, but it had also come back to strangle me! The rope was around my neck, and since the dinghy now contained hundreds of pounds of water, I felt as powerless as a Senator in the hands of a high-priced dominatrix. Every time I reached up to try and free myself, a wave would fling my hands from the grablines. I should have sensed that things were getting truly perilous when I began to focus less on my survival and more on all of the pretty, yellow-green bubbles around me.

But then I was saved by the bell - or should that be 'saved by the skillet?' I could suddenly hear Philomena clanging madly on her rusty frying pan. Now it is bad enough to be strangled and drowned by your own dinghy, but to suffer such humiliation while in front of an audience with a dirty, old skillet as the house orchestra was just too much. Enraged by this absurd embarrassment, I marshaled together all of the strength that I had accumulated from years of juggling bowling balls for a living, and made one, great final effort to break free of my dinghy. But I failed miserably.

However, the Sky Bosun, who apparently finds my ongoing antics amusing, decided to cut me some slack, both metaphorically and literally. For, a few seconds later, a wave really somersaulted us. But by flipping the dinghy over, it emptied out the water, which lightened it enough for me to free myself. I half swam and half got swept up to the beach. As I crawled the final yards out of the surf, cruisers were running down from the restaurant to help me. It is likely that nobody sitting with their margaritas enjoying my acrobatics in the black waves, had any idea of what extreme danger I had just escaped.

And as I panted on the wet sand, trying to regain my breath, it suddenly seemed to me that the tempo and tone of Phil's hammering had changed. It was no longer hammering an alert for everyone to watch my comic display. Instead, to my ears, it was singing a song of survival and victory. No sailor home from the sea had ever heard a sweeter and more triumphant song than the one Philomena was now playing on that rusty old skillet.

Sailing to Mombasa

Normal people might have found our display of bravado a bit strange. They might have felt that our devil-may-care attitudes were an attempt to repress hidden, deep-seated fears. But we were so far removed from normal, that we probably couldn't even spell it anymore. In fact, between our three, sea-roving sailboats we had two-and-a-half circumnavigations. We had been Out There with a capital O and a capital T. So to us it made perfect sense to pass the time during a ferocious electrical storm by telling first-person lightning stories.

We were seated in the saloon of a handsome Beneteau 50, which had just finished chartering its way around the world. Lots of folks make a living by running charters in one particular area, such as the Caribbean or the Med; but Captain Lars and Divemaster Johanna rejected that normal approach in favor of a more difficult but rewarding, globe-rounding itinerary. Through their own extensive contacts, they can fill the boat with up to six paying guests for much of the year. They supplement this with the help of Mary Crowley's adventure sail/travel company called Ocean Voyages. This Sausalito, California-based agency specializes in finding vessels for people who seek out-of-the-way places, from Zanzibar to Zamboanga. Anybody savvy enough to charter aboard *Jennifer* would soon find themselves under the spell of two pretty amazing sea gypsies.

Lars is a reformed lawyer and an unreformed vagabond. He has traveled around the world twice. Along the way he would trek, ski, climb mountains, scuba dive, run marathons, and teach aerobics. He was born in Sweden and took his Master's degree in law at the University of Illinois. So his English is better than that of half the Senate and the entire House. He is also a damned fine captain who believes that good seamanship is proven by smooth, trouble-free passages.

Johanna refers to herself as Dutch Canadian. This threw me at first, because I was aware of French Canada and of the British part of Canada, but I didn't realize that there was a Dutch portion. Then she explained that she had been born in Holland, but spent much of her life in Canada. She has been a scuba devotee - or should that be dive-otee? - for a very long time. Her impressive resumé includes some pioneering cave dives in the Yucatan and owning a dive resort in Belize. She met Lars by thumbing rides on sailboats all the way from California to Mexico to the South Pacific. They've now been together for three years and three oceans.

The other couple seated in *Jennifer's* saloon had also left the norm far astern. They too had circumnavigated, and in a most unusual sloop. It had so many tools arrayed below, that it looked like the supply ship for a fleet of Mr. Goodwrenches. That's because Eric, the skipper, was a master mechanic, or, as he liked to describe himself, a 'master bleeder.' This referred to the main task that other cruisers hired him to perform, the mystic and secret ritual known as the 'bleeding of the diesel.'

His first mate, Audrey, was an excellent canvas worker. This had earned her the nickname of Canvas Audrey. However, because of her almost neurotic penchant for sewing covers for almost everything on the boat, she was sometimes called Compulsive Audrey. She had even made a cover for their main anchor. This must have added at least three days to the lifespan of this galvanized steel plow, which could already survive about 10,000 years before the sun began to damage it.

Eric and Audrey were from Australia. The name of their boat was from Mars. At least that was my first guess when I saw the word *Icfigin* painted across their stern. Then, when I saw the inside of their sloop, I thought that perhaps it was the brand name of an Australian torque wrench. Finally I just broke down and asked.

"Oh, it's an acronym," said Audrey, with a playful smile.

"It stands for, 'I Can Feel It Going In Now.' " added Eric with an equally naughty smile.

So, I guess it had something to do with fuel injection or pistons.

Well, as I previously mentioned, we were seated in the saloon of a handsome Beneteau 50. What I didn't tell you was that it was docked at Marina Hemingway, a few miles west of Havana. There was a thunderstorm raging around us that was impressive by capitalist standards, but apparently this was just an average one by Cuban standards. That's because many of the workers at the marina kept claiming that this was the 'lightning capital of the world.'

Now I can recall at least three other ports in North and Central

America that have also claimed that title. So my conclusion was that this was the 'lightning capital of the communist world' which probably isn't that big a deal, since to the best of my knowledge, Cuba is the only communist country still left in the Western Hemisphere. Unless you count Berkeley.

After a particularly fierce lightning-and-thunder combo, Eric said, "Hey, have I got a great lightning story for you guys. You're all familiar with Fosters Beer aren't you?"

"More than we should probably admit to," came the consensus reply.

"Well, *Icfigin* was sailing from Fiji to New Zealand and ..."

At this point Audrey interrupted. "Eric, the story would be even better if you showed them the Glob."

"Great idea," he said, as he quickly climbed up the companionway ladder and headed to their boat, which was berthed just behind *Jennifer* and directly in front of *Aventura*.

"He'll get drenched," said Johanna, in mild disbelief.

"Ah, no worries, Jo," said Audrey. "He's a true Aussie. He thinks that since we're in the Northern Hemisphere, the rain flows up."

He soon returned bearing a large metallic blob. Looking at it, I was reminded of a friend's theory: 'If you don't know what something is, it's probably art.' So my guess was that it was either chrome-plated road kill... or sculpture. Well, it turned out to be a work of art created by the Sky Bosun himself. Because on that trip from Fiji to New Zealand, Eric and Audrey had an entire case of Fosters stowed in the bilge. During a strong thunderstorm, they thought they had taken a direct lightning hit, because the cabin lights went out a second after they saw a blinding flash. But they came back on in a few seconds, and they could here the autopilot whirring away as it made course adjustments out in the cockpit. So they figured it was just another near miss.

Later that afternoon, Eric opened the bilge to get a few brews to transfer to the fridge. What he saw was a true male Aussie nightmare. His entire supply of Fosters was destroyed. The lightning had come down the mast, evaporated the beer, and melted the cans into a pelican-sized glob of blue and silver metal. His impassioned curses could probably be heard in both Fiji and New Zealand. And it didn't matter whether you were Down Under or Up Over; they could be easily understood.

Audrey tried to calm him down by pointing out that the sacrificial beer had probably kept all of their electronics from being destroyed. "Screw the GPS!" he replied. "I can navigate with my sextant, but I can't drink melted aluminum."

Eventually, Audrey managed to calm him down by suggesting that they make something positive out of this molten negative. After all, they had that big space on the main bulkhead that needed something decorative; so rather than imbibing the Fosters, they could immortalize it. This is consistent with much of modern art in that what ends up on the wall looks a lot like something that went wrong.

"So, is that a great lightning story, or what?" asked Eric.

"Pretty good," replied Johanna, "but I think Lars can top it."

"You're kidding?" said Audrey.

"Oh, it's no joke," responded Lars.

"Come on, Lars, tell them," urged Johanna.

"All right. Well, we were sailing to Mombasa…"

"Wait. Stop right there, mate," protested Eric. "You can't bloody start a story with 'We were sailing to Mombasa.' Do you think you're Joseph Conrad or something?"

"OK, OK. We were actually sailing to Kalifi, which is very near Mombasa on the coast of Kenya. We were sailing there

141

because Tony from the ham radio net, which stretches all across the Indian Ocean and up the Red Sea, lives there. After having spoken with him by radio so often, we wanted to meet him. But to get to his place you had to go up a river. And to go up that particular river you had to pass under a bridge and under some high-tension power lines."

"Other cruisers from that area had told us that we would have no trouble clearing those obstacles. But they failed to tell us something very critical, namely, that you couldn't steer the obvious course. The highest part of the bridge was in the middle of the river, but the power lines were slightly higher over by the right-hand bank. Unfortunately, this is not apparent to someone approaching from mid-channel."

At this point Johanna picked up the tale. "So I was up on the foredeck, trying to judge if our mast would clear the wires. There were three of them about 30 feet apart. The middle one had some weights or conductors or something on it. They looked like big heavy balls and made this one hang down the lowest. We cleared the first one OK, and as we eased forward, ever so slowly, it looked like we would miss the second one. And indeed we did. So now I thought that we were home free. But as we got closer to the last one, I thought it looked too iffy, so I let go of the headstay and ran back toward the cockpit and told Lars to throw it into reverse"

"Which I did," continued Lars, "because from my perspective it also looked too close. But before I could get the boat stopped, we hit it. People standing on the shore later told us that they saw a blue bolt of electricity travel down the headstay and arc into the water at the bow. But some of it came my direction too. My hand was on the metal throttle lever and this huge charge of current just started surging through my body. After a few seconds it jolted me back against the stern railing where I could now feel the electricity

142

rushing up and down my body. I thought I was dead meat - very well done dead meat."

"But then the boat, which was still in reverse, must have freed itself from the wire. The current released me from where it had pinned me, and I stumbled forward on to one of the cockpit benches. It would be a while before I left that spot."

"A while?" chuckled Johanna. "Try a week! The electricity had injured him so severely that he couldn't move from there for an entire week. It was so extreme that I had to feed him and bathe him and attend to, shall we say, less pleasing needs. I built a screen all the way around the cockpit out of clear plastic to keep out the rain and bugs. He literally couldn't move."

"But I'm getting ahead of myself in the story," she continued. "I backed the boat clear of the wires and then put out a *Mayday* call on the radio. Some nearby cruisers came racing out in their dinghies. One of them raced back and got a doctor. I had already given him a muscle relaxant and a Valium, and when the doctor got there he did a very careful examination. Just like I had secretly done, he was looking for an exit wound where the current might have come out."

"I told the doctor that it probably blasted out through his hair because when I first saw him stuck against the stern rail, his normally wavy locks were sticking straight up, just like in the cartoons. With that jock's body of his, he looked like a cross between Einstein and an aerobics teacher. The fact that Lars could wiggle his fingers and toes was a good sign. This meant that he had suffered no permanent spinal or nerve damage. Essentially, he had just sustained extreme muscle trauma caused by the voltage ripping through him. So even the slightest attempted movement caused big groups of muscles to cramp up, which meant excruciating pain. Once the doctor assured me that he would be OK, and that he just needed rest and immobilization, I felt a lot better."

"Then, with the help of some of the other cruisers, I moved *Jennifer* into the anchorage, using the proper route. It turns out that you have to come down the river mid-channel until you're near the wires and then zig over to the right bank and pass under them there. Once clear, you zag back to the middle of the channel again in order to clear the bridge. How everybody could fail to mention the all-important zig-zag part seemed pretty negligent to me, but I was feeling so good about the fact that Lars was OK that I didn't press the issue."

"It was a whole week before I could even sit up." said Lars, taking over the narrative again. "I know it was difficult for Jo having to wait on me day and night, but for a lifelong athlete like myself it was pure hell being stuck there like that. After I could finally move without my system going into panic and cramp mode, it took another 10 days before I regained full mobility and a couple of months before I felt like my real self."

"Were there any long-term effects?" asked Audrey with a smile and a wink. "Did any of his parts glow silver-blue in the darkness?"

"Not any more than it used to," replied Johanna as the male skippers chuckled. "And he didn't lose his sense of humor either. In fact as we were motoring out of there a month later he was wearing huge oven mitts as we passed under the wires."

"Bravo, mate," said Eric. "But how can you claim that your lightning story is better than mine, since yours is actually an electrocution story?"

"Well, that's the beauty of it, Eric," answered Lars, "because a month earlier I had installed one of those anti-lightning devices at the top of the mast. You know those metal spikey things that look like the hair on a punk rocker doll? Well, I had forgotten that it added another 10 inches to my boat height. So I almost got fried by man-made lightning through a device that's supposed to protect me from real lightning. Pretty ironic, wasn't it?"

"And pretty ionic, too," said Johanna.

"But I bet you learned your lesson," commented Eric. "And I bet you keep a good damned eye on that spikey fellow when you go underneath something now, don't you?"

"Oh, not really," said Lars with exaggerated nonchalance.

"Why not?" asked Audrey.

"Look behind you." answered Johanna.

And there mounted on the main bulkhead was 'the metal spikey thing' with a silver frame around it.

Admiral Macaroon

I always bring my balls to a cruisers' potluck dinner. It's the sensible thing to do for two reasons. First, I have been a professional juggler for over 20 years. And second, I have been a pathetic cook for over 30 years. The other sailors in the Mexican cruising fleet always seemed to enjoy my juggling performances and some were quite memorable for me as well.

For example, there was the Christmas party at a sailor's bar in Cabo San Lucas at the southern tip of Mexico's Baja peninsula. The owners of the place had tried to clear a space large enough to accommodate both my act and the audience, but I was nervous. I was feeling claustrophobic, and it wasn't Santa Claustrophobic. That's because the 20 cruising kids sitting up front were way too close. And the difference between a close call and a 911 call is marginal for a juggler of torches, hatchets, sickles, machetes, and bowling balls.

Besides, I really liked these junior sailors. Indeed, one of the true joys of the sea-gypsy life is meeting the terrific cruising kids. Unlike the brats, jive artists, and bullies that seem to dominate the adolescent scene in the so-called real world, most of these young voyagers are bright, cheerful, polite, healthy, curious, and eager to help each other. Because of this, I was very fond of these kids and I didn't want to fondue any of them.

My first routine went very well, but when I lit the torches to begin my fire juggling, the anxiety level of the crowd suddenly increased to Force 9. I couldn't quite fathom why everyone was so nervous until someone hollered, "Watch out for the blimp, Ray!"

Then I spotted the large, blow-up plastic dirigible suspended above me. It was an advertising gimmick for a beer company, and I couldn't believe that I hadn't noticed it on my own. But perhaps that was because I was blinded by the psychedelically bright Christmas piñatas dangling from other parts of the ceiling. While visions of Hindenburgs danced in my head, I juggled the torches as carefully as possible. It was imperative that I not make a mistake or I'd have to suffer two gruesome consequences. First, the plastic blimp would be horribly engulfed in flames and come cascading down onto the cruising kids. And second, some wiseguy would surely blurt out, "I said I wanted a Bud light!"

But that was Christmas and this was Valentine's Day. And today's potluck was not being organized by cruisers. Instead, it was mostly a gathering of the U.S. and Canadian expatriates who swell the Mexican town of Barra de Navidad during the winter season. Since I couldn't bring my juggling act as my contribution to the festivities, and since my culinary skills are questionable, I decided to borrow a friend's Magic Eggs.

This friend, Dave, is a fellow singlehander whose potluck specialty is pickled eggs. Eight hard-boiled beauties hang suspended in a brine that has frightening similarity to a jar of holding tank 'fluid.' And if the noxious appearance of these huevos grossos in their large glass jar was not forbidding enough, you only needed to unscrew the lid to finalize your decision. When you regained consciousness, you had to admire the brilliance of my friend's strategy, in which he prepared one item that could last for dozens of potlucks. Unfortunately, he was not aboard when I rowed over to borrow his magic jar.

So I headed to town in search of some food that could serve as my offering. Almost effortlessly I found what seemed like the perfect item, a nice package of macaroons. There were about two dozen of the coconut candies in the box, and the price was very reasonable. Indeed, it was so affordable that it distracted me from noticing something important, namely, that I had purchased them in a shoe store. Back aboard *Aventura*, I removed the macaroons from their packaging, set a few aside, and then attempted to make them look homemade by wrapping them in aluminum foil.

Two of my favorite cruising couples shared a cab with me from Melaque to Barra. We were amazed by the turnout for the dinner. Apparently the Valentine's Day Potluck is *the* social event of the season for the Norteamericanos who make Barra de Navidad their winter home. There were about 200 of the townies present, and they were decked out in technicolor, tropical finery. Beautiful, bright flowery dresses were favored by the women, while the men opted for pale linen suits and Panama hats. If Jimmy Buffet had snuck into town to be secretly married, this would surely have been his wedding reception.

The setting was pure Mexican Riviera, a lovely stucco-and-tile hotel that overlooked an unspoiled lagoon. The centerpiece was a garden that was enormous and luxuriant. Also adding to the ambiance were cavorting monkeys and exotic birds. I swear that one of the parrots had even been trained to deliver subliminal messages such as "Polly want a - margaritas half-price - cracker." With a poolside bar, mariachis, and banana trees, it was a splendid setting. A large portion of the garden had been cordoned off and reserved for the party. Noticing this, I concluded that these people took their potlucks seriously. I didn't know the half of it.

We were all marshaled into a long line and the admittance process began. I positioned myself in front of a superbly beautiful woman. This was imperative, because the other eight cruisers, who were coupled off, had been teasing me about being the only person at a Valentine's party without a date. So I felt obligated to defend the honor of singlehanded sailors in general, and heterosexual San Francisco bachelors in particular.

My new friend, Leah, was a gorgeous bearer of ugly tidings. She explained to me that this was no ordinary potluck, but rather a gourmet feast. In fact, it was a cooking competition with valuable prizes awarded to the most delicious and artistic dishes. Furthermore, since it was acknowledged as the finest banquet of the entire year in all of Barra de Navidad, the organizers were adamant that everyone should bring only homemade delicacies, lest the event be infiltrated by freeloaders. Leah told me all of this with a discernible twinkle in one eye. Her other eye was focused on my humble, store-bought macaroons, hidden beneath their aluminum foil camouflage. She then lifted her entry closer to my nose and asked, "Do you like my Tuna Tartare?"

"Why yes; and it has a subtle but fragrant bouquet," I replied.

"And what indescribable delicacy are you hiding beneath that tin foil?" she inquired.

"Why spoil a superb surprise?" I answered.

But it wouldn't be a mystery for long, since the line was moving quickly, and we were rapidly approaching the entrance station. Three people were positioned there, and they seemed to be taking their duties very seriously. In fact, it appeared that crossing a Golan Heights checkpoint disguised as Yassar Arafat, would be easier than running this gauntlet. A PSO (Potluck Surveillance Officer) recorded my name, assigned me a number and asked which division I would be entering.

"Desserts," I replied.

"And what special sweets have you prepared for us?"

I peeled back the aluminum foil. Then the stunned and disbelieving PSO blurted out, "Macaroons?"

A hush descended. I was dumbfounded. Admittedly, I wasn't anticipating an enthusiastic response to my modest candies, but this appalled silence was most unsettling. It was as if I had presented them with a Preparation H casserole. The highest-ranking PSO then took a small but deliberate step toward me and initiated eye contact. Then he asked in a stern and solemn voice, "Did you bake these macaroons?!"

The silence deepened. All ears awaited my response. How could I succinctly tell this potluck vigilante that I had no idea that their dinner was such a big deal; that at other such gatherings I had always given generously of my juggling talents; that I was a terrible cook; and that I thought I was doing everyone a favor by not attempting to prepare something myself. Since I couldn't say that in 25 words or less, I looked my interrogator directly in the eye and replied confidently, "I cannot tell a lie. YES, I baked these macaroons!"

Upon my pronouncement, beautiful Leah went into hysterics. She laughed and cackled and guffawed with unbridled gusto.

Although I was not exactly delighted by her robust sense of humor, it apparently saved me. Realizing that I had already suffered enough embarrassment by her outburst, the officials allowed me to enter on the condition that my macaroons must be a non-juried entry.

A few minutes later, I asked Leah as diplomatically as possible why she had cracked up so exuberantly over my macaroons. She proceeded to explain to me that they were absolutely everywhere in Barra de Navidad. In fact, you couldn't go anywhere in town without finding a few packages of them for sale next to the cash register. She thought that they might have something to do with charities, like our Girl Scout cookies, but she wasn't certain. So in a town famous for its happy hours, it was actually easier to find macaroons than margaritas.

But ironically these macaroons were just as effective as margaritas because they began a close and special friendship between Leah and me that continues to this day. We had a terrific time at the party, and made a date for her to visit *Aventura* the next day. Apparently, word of this rendezvous quickly spread through the cruising fleet. This was evident because as we walked the beach, I could frequently see the glint of sunlight bouncing off binoculars out in the anchorage. This was understandable because Leah sewed her own bikinis and refused to waste material by using too much on one suit. In fact, you could probably fit six of them in a blender.

During our sumptuous V-berth interlude, which followed our stroll on the shore, I would periodically poke my head out of the forehatch and note that the binocular gleams were still there. This amused us enormously; so we decided to reward our voyeurs for their patience. We went topside and sat on the cabin with our backs against the mast. I was wearing my skimpiest speedos and Leah was adorned in nothing but her tiny thong. In the deep, rich amber light of late afternoon on the Mexican Riviera, we must have looked golden and euphoric. But one thing seemed out of place in this idyllic scene. Why were we laughing lustily as we fed each other macaroons?

Doctor Stingray

Perhaps it was just the exotic setting, but I swear that her eyes had an otherworldly glow. They were like turquoise fire on a moonless night. And they seemed that extraordinary to me even before I heard the story of Doctor Stingray.

When I first met her she was a land pioneer, but it was her many years as a sea pioneer that had drawn me across the wide bay to visit her homestead. For 40 years, Maggie and her husband Patrick had lived aboard their stout but graceful wooden ketch. They had wandered the Seven Seas (or, as she liked to call them, the Severe Seas) when small-craft cruising was in its infancy. They would often share anchorages with the Hiscocks and Smeetons, as they were carving and covering their famous wakes.

When the hills of Fiddler's Green began to beckon Patrick, they decided that the boat would be too much for Maggie to handle alone. So they sold their ketch and bought a few acres on the shores of the Gulf of Nicoya, in Costa Rica. There, during his final year, they adapted their rugged, self-reliant sea skills to building a simple but secure homestead. The lighting was kerosene, the cooking was wood, the water was well.

After her husband set his final anchor, Maggie lived alone for a year. But all of those close-quarter years of marriage and voyaging made living in total isolation too difficult. So she sold part of her property to some friends who built a cabin close by, insuring her some companionship. After that, her days were peacefully filled with rustic enjoyments: baking bread, reading, beachcombing, and enjoying the chatter of the howler monkeys.

I visited Maggie on a cloudy day just before sunset and just after a fierce lightning storm. Perhaps it was this meteorological timing that caused her eyes to shine so vibrantly. We drank tea and ate some of her homemade bread. She told lovely tales from her days at sea with Patrick. But I could sense that this flood of memories was too heart-rending for her. So I changed the subject to… kerosene.

I asked if the beautiful lamps in her cabin were from their old boat. She said yes, and lit one for me. The mellow glow and fragrant smell was soothing to both of us. I mentioned that my boat cabin was also lit by kerosene lamps, and that I loved the warm, amber light, even though it wasn't bright enough for me to read by.

She surprised me by saying that she read by it and that was a good thing because books were a major joy in her life. "But a year ago my eyes had gotten so bad that I had to use very strong eyeglasses," she continued. "And they kept getting worse. I was about to buy an electric lamp when Doctor Stingray helped me."

My initial thought was that Doctor Stingray was probably some eccentric, crystal-swinging, herbal-compressing acupuncturist whose name indicated that he also suffered from comic-book delusions. So naturally, I asked about him.

"Oh, no, no," she said. "It isn't a person - it's a healer from the sea. One day when I was beachcombing in the shallows I accidentally stepped on a big stingray and it stabbed me with its venomous spike, just above my ankle. I had been stung twice before, but they were smaller ones and I just cleaned the wound and bandaged it up. In a day or two it was barely noticeable."

"But this must have been a real grand-daddy. That night I woke up from a dream in which my foot was being amputated at the ankle. The reality was almost as bad; from the knee down, my leg was grotesquely swollen. Plus, it was dark gray and looking like it wanted to turn black. Fortunately, I was able to hobble over to my neighbor's cabin for help. They took one look at it and fired up the jeep. By the time we got to the Puntarenas hospital I had passed out."

"I woke up when the first needle hit my bum, but I quickly went back to sleep. How many shots I got in the next few days I'll never know, because many of them knocked me out. I'm sure there were at least a dozen. The reason for so many was because the doctors were having trouble figuring out just what medicine might cure me. My stern was black and blue for a week. It took five days for me to recover. Everybody at the hospital treated me so wonderfully. They brought me flowers and candy, and they even went out of their way to find me American magazines."

"One day while I was reading a magazine, a nurse came in with my breakfast. After she set down the tray, I asked her if she could hand me the case for my eyeglasses. As she was passing it to me, I reached up to take off my glasses and was surprised to discover that I wasn't wearing them! I looked back down at the magazine, expecting it to be blurry and impossible to read, but it was clear and easy to read. When I opened up the case, there were my glasses - unused."

"So you think that somehow the stingray's poison rejuvenated your failing eyes?" I asked.

"Who knows?" she said. "The doctors think that one of the medicines that they shot into me might have somehow restored my eyes to their youthful power."

But I wasn't convinced. For the turquoise flame of those eyes and that awesome vision seemed to me to be way beyond the power of modern medicine. Instead, I will always believe that those hypnotic eyes were a direct result of one injection of Doctor Stingray's Magic Elixir.

Without a Net

A thousand miles from the nearest land is a great place for philosophical reflection but a lousy place for visual reflection. Because
when you can lean over the side of your sleeping sloop and see
yourself with mirror-like clarity, you are Becalmed with a capital
B. The three previous days had also been completely windless and
now even the long, deep-ocean swell, what I like to call the Breathing of the Beast, had disappeared. From horizon to horizon the sea
was so eerily still and intensely blue that it seemed like the Sky
Bosun had decided to whip up a batch of Windex jello.

Usually, I find such surroundings soothing, but this time I was
seething. That's because a woman was waiting, a special woman.
We had met after one of my juggling shows at San Francisco's
finest street fair, the Union Street Festival. Christiane let the rest of
the crowd fill my hat and disperse before she came up to me. At

this time I didn't know that she modeled for fitness magazines, but the Lycra tank top and bicycle shorts should have tipped me off. Interestingly enough, her first words to me were precisely what I was thinking as she approached.

"Thank you."

"For what?" came my uncertain reply.

"For making me laugh so many times through the years."

She then placed a neatly folded lump of greenbacks into my hand and closed my fingers around them. While placing the bills in my pocket, I mumbled something inane like, "I'd rather have your phone number than your money."

To her immense credit she didn't give me her number. But we did have a pleasant, playful chat for a few minutes before she headed off for the booths and the bustle of the street fair. Several minutes later, while readying my props for the next show, I remembered her offering. When I removed it from my pocket, instead of the expected four or five dollars, I discovered five $20 bills.

Later that day Christiane paid me a return visit and I was able to thank her and suggest that we spend the $100 on a lovely dinner somewhere. On that first date, two of her little personality traits helped to win my everlasting affection. The first occurred at her apartment when she asked me to 'Thaw out some plastic.' When I replied that I didn't know what the fridge she was talking about, she instructed me to open the icebox and figure it out. There in the freezer I found three credit cards encased in ice in Ziploc bags. It was her clever way of restraining herself from using them too often.

At the restaurant, a second endearing trait revealed itself. She insisted that the maitre dí find us a table where we could sit beside each other, instead of across from each other. To an unreformed and unrepentant romantic like myself, this was a sublime gesture.

For the next month we had an exquisite time together until I had to depart on the Singlehanded TransPac to Hawaii. The race took me 20 days, followed by a few days of celebrating with the other skippers and a week preparing *Aventura* for the long, tough, up-wind trip home to San Francisco.

The return voyage turned into a contest also - a race for romance. Christiane was flying off with her parents to spend two weeks on a cruise ship in the Caribbean. They were leaving in 32 days. My last sail back from Hanalei Bay a few years before had taken 29 days. So there was no time to dawdle. And no time to waddle, which was about all that my sloop and I were doing on this windless water. I had motored slowly through the first three days of calms, but now only four gallons of diesel fuel remained. I had to save this small amount for my final approach to San Francisco, which can be very treacherous with the fog and the currents and the shipping.

Every four hours I would put out this radio message: "Any vessel, any vessel, any vessel - this is the sailboat *Aventura*. Can anyone read me?" No one could. At least for the first few days. And then suddenly there was a response to my broadcast. A wonderful, deep, 'Zorba the Greek' voice identified himself as the captain of a 700-foot bulk carrier and asked if I was in distress.

I replied that sloop and skipper were fine but that I could really use some weather info. Once the wind returned, I wanted to know what course to steer to find more of it. He asked for my position and went to check his weatherfax. He returned bearing bad tidings and even used American slang to express them.

"I have some bad news and some worse news. Do you want to hear it?"

"No, but I probably should."

"OK, here goes."

Where did he learn his shopping-mall English, I wondered to myself?

"The Pacific High Pressure Zone of no wind stretches from Hawaii to Alaska to Nevada. That's the bad news. The worse news is that your position is on the crossbar of the 'H' which marks the center of the High."

I groaned like a teenager on a date with an early curfew. This brought a sympathetic response from the master of the bulk carrier. "What's the problem?" he said.

I tried not to be distracted by his suburban slang delivered with an ouzo accent and replied, "My problem is that I've been becalmed for four days and have used all but my emergency fuel. I'm on a tight schedule to get back to San Francisco and it looks like I might not make it."

"There wouldn't happen to be a woman involved, would there?"

The Greeks have a long history of longing for the women they've left behind as they face the perils of the sea, so his intuition did not surprise me. "Indeed there would," came my honest reply.

"Well, maybe I can help you. We could give you some fuel."

Visions of my fuel injectors trying to pump his ship's fuel, which has the consistency of a Calistoga mud bath, into my little diesel were so unsettling that I was slow in responding to his generous offer. But finally I managed to say, "Thanks, but no thanks. Your fuel wouldn't work in my engine."

"Thanks, but no thanks. Hey, I like that one. Hold on while I write it down."

When he came back on the radio, he said that of course he wasn't going to give me his heavy bunker fuel, but instead some regular diesel fuel. They used it in some of their small generators.

His plan was to cross my bow and drop a few large plastic jerry jugs into the water. By not filling them completely, they retain sufficient buoyancy. I could then use some of my emergency fuel to motor over and pick them up. Captain Zorba, as I now thought of him, said that he had done this once before for a singlehander in the Indian Ocean. And since he now understood that I was impressed by his mastery of American idiom, he paused for dramatic effect before saying, "It worked like a charm!"

His generous offer of help had me so ecstatic that I couldn't have been any happier if the Swedish Bikini Team had been about to parachute in and gang massage me. The captain was obviously enjoying this break from their normal routine because his next transmission was, "Here we come, ready or not." A few minutes later he said that he had me on his radar six miles directly ahead. I looked astern but could see nothing on the tinted glass sea. Normally a ship that size should be visible at that distance. I chalked it up to haze on the horizon. His next radio message got me worrying a little.

"Why did you alter course to starboard?"

"I didn't alter course. My engine isn't even on yet. I'm just bobbing around."

Could the stillness and the heat have unknowingly put me to sleep so that I was daydreaming this entire incident? His next call made me pinch myself to insure that I was awake.

"Why did you turn to port? And why did you shoot off that orange smoke flare?"

"Captain," I said, "How many masts does my boat have?"

"Two," came his reply. This was also about the same distance in nautical miles that my spirits sank when I heard this news. Of course the crew of the poor little ketch that thought it was being stalked by a 700-foot ship probably felt emotions far more powerful than just disappointment. But since their radio obviously wasn't turned on or working, I never got to speak with them. Nor did I ever get to see Captain Zorba's ship. My celestial navigation for the last few days had been a bit nonchalant and I hadn't concerned myself too much with where the current was drifting me. So who knows where I actually was in relation to the big Greek carrier of not just bulk but kindness?

A little over a day later the wind returned. Most sailors will agree that the wind you get is usually either too much or not enough. I like to describe this phenomenon as either 'too passive or too massive.' And sure enough, it built from Force Nil to Force Shrill very quickly. But since I was in a hurry and since the wind was aft of the beam I poled out the jib, eased the main, hung on, and grinned. The ride was so wild and exhilarating that I started thinking of my stout little sloop as my RTV - my Rodeo Training Vehicle.

Every few hours I'd reduce sail, until by sunset a triple-reefed main was more than enough. With darkness coming, I needed to return the spinnaker pole to its secure position. The inboard end slides up a long track on the front of the mast and the outboard end clips into a chock at the base of the stick. The pole was now pulled against the portside of the headstay and firmly held there by the downhaul tension. I needed to release the sheet, which is sailor-speak for the rope, from the jaws of the pole so that it would be free to slide up the mast track. So, as I had done a hundred times before, I unhooked the cockpit tether that attaches to my safety harness and clipped on one of my foredeck tethers. These are deliberately longer so that I can work comfortably on either side of the bow.

Up at the headstay I reached up to pull the line that opens the jaws and frees the sheet. This is a tiptoe operation for me because the height of the pole is even with the top of my head. As I released the jib sheet, the boat suddenly lurched and I found myself hanging on for dear life, or wet death. Apparently the downhaul had let go because the pole had swung out over the water with me gripping it like the devil's own chin-up bar.

The first arc that it made was particularly memorable because the back of my thighs slammed into the stainless steel bow pulpit as I got carried out over the ocean. The end of that first arc was equally unforgettable, because what abruptly stopped it was the eight-foot tether attached to the harness in the middle of my chest. On its next swing back to the headstay, my knees slammed into the bow pulpit almost causing me to lose my grip. I was beginning to feel like the star in an action movie, except that there was no crew just out of range of the camera's eye to watch over me.

On about the fifth swing back and forth, my arm strength was just about gone, and I knew that if I wasn't soon decisive I would be soon deceased. So the next time that the pole careened back towards the bow, I let go and tried to dive back onto the foredeck. Olympic judges would probably have given me high marks for degree of difficulty but low marks for style. My right shoulder slammed into the starboard top of the bow pulpit just after my right anklebone slammed onto the portside top of the bow pulpit. Then my body jackknifed at the waist and bounced onto the foredeck. The final impact was my hipbone slugging the anchor windlass.

During the whole episode I have no recollection of being terrified, but as soon as my body came to rest, I started shaking uncontrollably. In order to regain my composure, I had to wrap myself around the windlass in the fetal position and gradually slow down my breathing and my sobbing. For I was certain that had I lost my grip and fallen into the sea, I would not have been able to pull myself back aboard. The flare of the bow, the height of the topsides and the speed of the boat would have made it nearly impossible. My only chance would have been to unhook my tether and try to work my way aft where the boat is lower and attempt to pull myself aboard. More likely, I would have been dragged along to a slow, grim death attached to my beloved *Aventura*.

But unless this is being ghost written, that did not happen. In fact, the whole story has a happy ending, because I made it back to Christiane with two days to spare. When I eased my boat into the Pier 39 marina, she and about 10 other friends were there with champagne and smiles to celebrate my return. Many toasts were made and when it was my turn to make one I raised my glass and said, "To my bowling balls!" This might have sounded like an off-the-wall toast but it was quite sincere, because if I had not spent 10 years juggling them, I might not have had the strength to survive my recent ordeal.

Naturally, my friends were a bit curious about my rather odd toast, and so I told them the story. Just as I have now told you the story.

High Seas Master

Crossing the finish line of the Singlehanded TransPac was exquisite. Finding the finish line of the Singlehanded TransPac was excruciating. At the final skippers' meeting, the race committee had briefed us on weather patterns, emergency radio frequencies, and starting-line penalties. But somehow they forgot to brief us on Charo.

Now don't try to tell me that you don't know who she is. Because I know that you know that she is that multi-talented star of stage and screen, that singer, guitarist, dancer, and actress, that 'koochie-koochie' gal, and, more importantly to this story, that budding restaurateur. Her new eatery at Hanalei Bay on Kauai just happened to be directly behind the SHTP finish line. What made this dangerous was the fact that she had chosen a nautical motif for her decor, which included bright port and starboard lights on her beachside patio.

Since the green light on the finish-line buoy is very similar to the green light on her palapa deck, it made for some heart-pounding navigation. One mistake and you'd be crunching coral, while Charo giggled 'koochie-koochie' from her patio. If your arrival happened to be in daylight, this was not a problem, because the difference between a buoy and a restaurant is fairly obvious.

So, naturally my finish was at night. There was a lot of haze near the entrance to Hanalei Bay as I made my final approach. Whether this was actually due to the nearness of Puff the Magic Dragon, who reportedly resided nearby in a gated community, I was never able to confirm. But I can assure you that the green light that I was searching for seemed to keep changing position. Since I wasn't even aware of the existence of Charo's restaurant, and since the race committee wasn't allowed to clarify my confusion, I closed out the 20th day of my sleep-deprived but excitement-filled race in nerve-racking fashion.

I didn't have GPS or radar to verify my position, but my coastal piloting skills eventually guided me safely to the correct green light. I suspect that if I had actually been bearing down on Charo's boat-hungry reef, the race committee would have warned me before *Aventura* and I became the Catch of the Day.

Once I had rounded the mark and officially finished the race, things turned golden. A big inflatable dinghy with a powerful engine roared out to me, and three race committee members shouted congratulations as they climbed aboard. First they ascertained that the seal on my prop shaft had not been broken. This indicated that my engine had only been used to charge my batteries and not to provide propulsion. Once this was established, they dropped and folded my sails, motored me into the bay, set my anchor and took me ashore to party.

And what a wonderful party it was. Before the race, each skipper gets to choose a beverage that will be awaiting him at the finish. My selection had been a six-pack of Anchor Steam Beer. Arriving at the beach, I was greeted by a large, boisterous group of fellow racers, along with their families and friends. A beautiful woman stepped out of the crowd and draped a plumeria lei around my neck. Then a less-than-beautiful multihull skipper handed me a cold, delicious bottle of Anchor Steam, a brew that dates back to clipper ship days and has the stoutness that you would expect from such lineage.

There were cheers, toasts and good-natured teasing from all of these people for whom I cared so much. Stories were told, stupid actions were laughed about, the windless Pacific High was cursed, spinnaker wraps were rewound and unwound and for one brief moment during that long and glorious reunion, I think that the truth might have even been distorted.

It was a night of special magnificence, a night to revel in challenges accepted and goals achieved, a night of such shining luminosity that its afterglow has helped me through some dark and difficult times since then. It was also a night to sleep. After almost three full weeks of catnapping in 20-minute segments, I was ready for some serious slumber. One of the best and nicest racers had rented a house on the beach. He generously let me sleep there that night and even though I still woke up every 20 minutes, it was glorious to not have to go topside to scan the horizon.

The next morning I borrowed a dinghy to row out to *Aventura*. Halfway there I was hailed by one of my favorite skippers from any race or any ocean. He hadn't been ashore for my arrival party because he is rather shy and not too comfortable in crowds. I had really been looking forward to seeing him again because I respected his seamanship and boat handling so much. He had done well in the race and when I congratulated him, he shrugged it off with his customary modesty, claiming that he just got lucky. We had a delightful time chatting for about 30 minutes and then I popped the question that I had been formulating for over 2,000 solo miles.

"Hans, I just couldn't balance my boat to keep her from rolling in those big, tradewind seas. I tried every possible sail combination, and I shifted weight to all sorts of positions on the boat. But I just couldn't keep her from corkscrewing down the waves. Is there any way to deal with the rolling - is there some secret that is eluding me?"

"Yes," he replied, "there is indeed."

Then he drew a little closer to me. He leaned slightly forward. And with a serious but peaceful look on his face he said, "The secret is simple. You must learn to *LOVE* the rolling."